THE CARRY HOME

the
CARRY HOME

LESSONS *from the* **AMERICAN WILDERNESS**

GARY FERGUSON

COUNTERPOINT

BERKELEY

Copyright © 2014 Gary Ferguson

All rights reserved under International and Pan-American Copyright
Conventions. No part of this book may be used or reproduced in any manner
whatsoever without written permission from the publisher, except in the case
of brief quotations embodied in critical articles and reviews.

Library of Congress Cataloging-in-Publication Data

Ferguson, Gary, 1956-
The Carry Home / Gary Ferguson.
pages cm
ISBN 978-1-61902-448-9 (hardback)
1. Nature—Psychological aspects. 2. Grief. 3. Bereavement. I. Title.

BF353.5.N37F47 2014
818'.5403—dc23
[B]

2014014428

ISBN 978-1-61902-448-9

Cover design by Gerilyn Attebery
Interior design by Domini Dragoone

Counterpoint Press
2560 9th St, Ste 318,
Berkeley, CA 94710
www.counterpointpress.com

Printed in the United States of America
Distributed by Publishers Group West

10 9 8 7 6 5 4 3 2 1

Wild geese fly over head.
They wrench my heart.
They were our friends in the old days.

—Li Ch'ing Chao, translated by Kenneth Rexroth

TABLE OF CONTENTS

THE CARRY HOME

AT FIRST

The end came for Jane, and so for us, at the edge of spring, when the leaves of the north country were washed in that impossible shade of lemonade green. A color she said always reminded her of a certain crayon in the old Crayola 64 boxes she had as a kid—one labeled simply "yellow green"—a clumsy name with no hint of the promise it held, which was like an early thought of summer before summer gets quickened by the sun. I was struck by how easily, how routinely she made such connections, coupling little shards of nature she found as an adult to some encounter when she was young. For her, then, wild country was a way in—a means of inciting the sweet startle of childhood.

Over our twenty-five years together, I came to learn such magic, too.

But with her death on the Kopka River, I was suddenly senseless, trying to remember how it all works. I'd find myself in some early memory of my own, when nature was first nudging my heart. But the memory was brittle, like a great creature gone extinct, surviving only in some museum exhibit—a Javan tiger, an Atlas bear. Something formerly amazing, but now just a stiff swatch of fur propped up behind a pane of glass. And I doubted the world could spin out something so compelling ever again.

* * * *

WE WERE BORN AT THE BACK FORTY OF THE BABY BOOM, IN THE corn and the rust; Jane in the farm country of southern Indiana, me in the blue-collar bricks and smokestacks of the North. Like a million other kids, we ended up squeezing our halcyon days out of loose meanderings through flutters of nature—city parks and stray wood lots, cattail marshes and hedgerows and creek banks. Living spring through fall with wind-tossed hair and dirty feet.

Only later did we come to realize the extent to which we'd been wandering in jagged, reckless times—times when nature was going to ruin. As I was climbing up sugar maples along the sidewalks of South Bend, Indiana, forty-five minutes to the west, near the town of Gary, U.S. Steel was every day dumping seventy-five tons of oil, ammonia, mercury, phenols, and cyanide into the Calumet River. Before long, it started catching fire. Women living near that river, mostly poor African-American women, were in the 1960s and '70s giving birth to babies deformed by mercury poisoning. Meanwhile their husbands and brothers and fathers and sons were coming home every day from working at the steel plants, stopping in some worn patch of grass outside the back door to spit dark spatters of coke dust.

By 1964 my brother and I could be found knotting hickory sticks into toy boats with pieces of string, then tossing them into lines of ditch water sheeted with DDT. To this day I can recall that certain sweet, heavy tang that hung in the air every spring— the smell of dioxin and phenols—some of it coming from the corn fields around town, more still oozing from the boat channels to the southeast, where we sometimes went swimming. Meanwhile, north of where we lived, at a Dow plant in Midland, Michigan, those same chemicals were being mixed with jet fuel, poured into fifty-five-gallon drums, and shipped to Vietnam as Agent Orange.

Down in the southern part of the state, where Jane lived, nature wasn't faring all that much better. During her senior year of high school, Secretary of Agriculture Earl Butz arrived at her family's farm, announcing to the Stewarts and their neighbors that the time had come to plant "fence row to fence row." It would take just two years for the last corners of mystery and modest disorder in that part of rural Indiana—those fabled Midwestern hedgerows, final holdouts for the fox and hooded warbler and raccoon—to all but disappear, plowed under to make way for still more corn and soybeans. One day out with Jane's dad on a slow drive around the farm, I listened to him tell how the wildlife he'd hunted as a boy to put food on the table had nearly vanished. Turkeys, opossums, game birds. Mostly gone.

"Get big," Earl Butz said to him in 1973. "Or get out."

* * * *

FOREMOST ON OUR MINDS IN THOSE YEARS WAS THE HOPE that the last of America's big, unfettered landscapes might help us sustain the openheartedness of youth; that encounters with the wild might yield some measure of light we could use to clarify a path through adulthood. We figured there were still lots of places where such things could happen: in the hickory hills of the Appalachians, or the jack pine of the North Woods. In the ice-blasted granite crags of northern New England, or the big redwoods of the West Coast. And if not there, then surely in the sagebrush deserts and aspen forests, the fast-dancing rivers and wind-blasted peaks of the Rockies.

A lot of our optimism was fed by the fact that, despite the brutal assault on nature going on when we were young—indeed, maybe because of it—there'd come on its heels an unqualified explosion of green reverie. We were eight years old when Congress passed the Wilderness Act—enshrining the hugely radical idea that land had intrinsic worth beyond what humans could extract from it—doing so with a unanimous vote in the Senate and only a single dissent in the House. Six years later, U.S. Senator Gaylord Nelson unfurled Earth Day, drawing some twenty million people into the nation's streets and parks to show a little love for the home planet. Soon Richard Nixon would establish the Environmental Protection Agency, and not long afterward, he'd put his signing pen to the Clean Air Act, the Clean Water Act, the National Environmental Protection Act.

By the time we entered high school in 1970, the outdoor education movement was exploding, along with hundreds of adventure programs like the National Outdoor Leadership School and Outward Bound. And from Oregon to North Carolina, California to Tennessee, thousands of young back-to-the-landers were running for the hills with copies of the *Whole Earth Catalog* or Bradford Angier's *We Like it Wild* stuffed into their packs, about to run out a stupendously naive, utterly spectacular quest to find some way to live closer to ground. All of it playing against a soundtrack of Canned Heat's "Going Up the Country," Marvin Gaye, with his melancholy lament for the state of the planet in "Mercy Mercy Me," Neil Young, droning in that eerie falsetto about mother nature being on the run in the 1970s.

* * * *

CURIOUSLY, THIRTY YEARS BEFORE WE WERE BORN, ANOTHER Hoosier from South Bend, a young Beat poet named Kenneth Rexroth, took a good look around the Midwest and shook his head. There was nothing left in the way of mythology, he grumbled. Nothing to take the place "of the gods and goddesses and heroes and demigods of the ancient world." With the curl and whim of that gone from our lives, Rexroth suggested, what we were mostly left with was a conspicuous, gnawing hunger to consume. What's more, he said, if imagination was ever to really flower again, if we wanted stories powerful enough to keep us awake, it would mean reimagining our connections to nature.

REXROTH WASN'T TRYING TO BRING BACK APOLLO AND Hermes and Dionysus; he was just pushing for the return of minds big enough, boisterous and generous and unruly enough to imagine them in the first place. Minds intrigued enough to midwife new versions of everything from technology to art, scholarship to love.

Rexroth would leave Indiana as a young adult, rolling west. He first came to rest in the Rocky Mountains, then the Pacific Northwest, and finally California, there climbing the Coast Range and the Sierras and writing poetry and drinking red wine into the wee hours with the likes of Allen Ginsberg and Gary Snyder. An accomplished poet himself, in time he became known far and wide as "the father of the Beats." He was happiest when moving: rolling down blue highways, huffing up mountain trails, moseying along lonely stretches of Pacific shoreline.

"See life steadily," he advised. "See it whole." Let the years be paced by the comings and goings of the seasons. What's more, learn to see that each of these seasons lives in all the others—winter in the blooms of summer, spring in the fading leaves of fall.

As it happened, my first chance to "see life steadily, see it whole," would come in the summer Jane and I married, working for the Forest Service, living in a tiny rust-red cabin not three hundred feet square on the bank of the Salmon River, in the Sawtooth Mountains of Idaho. The doorjambs and floorboards of the little cottage had gone crooked as a coyote's hind leg from sixty years of frost heaves. Out front was a tiny weathered porch, so tilted that the owner of the place—a seventy-five-year-old former sheepherder and aspiring Rube Goldberg impersonator named Stan Jenkins—cut short the two side legs of a chair to make it possible to sit without tipping over. Pleased with that success, he next set about fitting the two lone kitchen cabinets with screen-door hook-and-eye devices to keep the doors from swinging open.

The place had no sink, no running water. Dishes and other washing, beyond daily plunges in the river, we managed out of a large metal pan hung from a ten-penny nail on the kitchen wall. The toilet was forty yards away, in the corner of an off-kilter mouse-gray barn. Directly above the open rear tank of the commode, a faucet and pipe dropped from a large metal drum balanced in the rafters, which was filled by a hundred feet of garden hose attached to a small electric pump submerged at the edge of the river. Toilet visits were anxious, as we were always looking up, trying to gauge the general soundness of the cracked sheet of plywood Stan used to hold the drum.

Inside the cabin, without getting up from the edge of the old iron bed, we could reach the table, door, closet, and 1950 Frigidaire. A cracked Formica dining table drooped under the west window, where we ate bean burritos and looked out onto the river, not fifteen feet away, and beyond that to the rugged face of the Sawtooths shouting at the sky. Across the room, under the one other window, I cobbled together a desk from scraps of wood lying about the ranch, where I sat in the dim light of evening and wrote about the day.

Something good was in play for us along that wild river. Something in the sky, in meadows lit with paintbrush and prairie smoke and cinquefoil. It was an incomprehensibly big, soaring backdrop, and not a day went by when it didn't throw off sparks. We were opened up in that open country, suddenly able to think beyond corn and rust, navigating our days by following whatever whims of curiosity the land ignited.

And yet ours was never a story about the two of us all alone in the great wide open. There was deep community in that middle of nowhere, a knitting together of both old timers and newcomers, as animated as the land itself: endless potlucks and midnight fires; endless nights making music and days with friends riding inner tubes down the river or trekking up trails into the heart of the mountains. All of us out there riding on the backs of some earnest, footloose search for something striking, something beautiful. We romped without structure or intent, jumping into lakes and climbing rocks and sliding down snowfields on clean impulse. Kid play, really. Tasty as chocolate pudding.

A mile away from our little cabin, on a dirt street in the heart of Stanley, Idaho, was the Casino Club, where every August dozens of young singles planning to stay the winter in that frigid valley came together to kick off what was known as the mating season. With every passing week, they'd drink and dance across the gritty hardwood floors with growing urgency, more desperate as the month wore on to find a tolerable partner to help split wood and warm the sheets without driving each other crazy before spring broke the following May. Often it didn't work out that way—I mean the part about not driving each other crazy—and on the summer nights that followed, we'd sit drinking beer in the hot springs along the Salmon River, listening to those who'd spent the cold months tell of fiery breakups and cabin swaps; of forty-below nights when cars froze up outside Casanova Jacks, leaving everyone to sleep on the floor of the bar on a bed of beer cans and peanut shells. Or tales about the day the sheriff—said to be wrestling with relationship troubles of his own—highcentered his snow machine on a lodgepole pine behind the ranger station, then, in a fit of rage, pulled out his pistol and shot the tree in half.

It wasn't life out of balance but, rather, life brilliantly off balance. Those big lands—and just as important, what such places did to the people who lived there—helped us realize that we'd likely never really know what made either people or places tick. We were all wild, all mysterious, all worth a closer look.

At the time, Jane and I might've described ourselves as an eager teacher and an impatient science writer, both hungry for open ground. But in those mountains, we came to understand that the edges and overlays of people's lives, including our own, would be forever changing—sometimes slowly, like the seasons, and sometimes like May flood or August fire. Freedom, and we had freedom in spades, came from not needing to know what was next.

Following our time in the Sawtooths, the characters kept on coming: at a cowboy line camp we took care of deep in the aspen woods of northern Arizona; at the feet of the San Juan Mountains in southwest Colorado; and finally, in the last place we called home, on the ragged, rugged edges of greater Yellowstone. There was the brilliant, prodigal mountain town pianist, sitting in his tiny apartment fondling the keys of a grand piano like some poor man's Horowitz through the long days of winter, wearing fingerless gloves and nipping brandy because he had no money for heat. There were ski bums from L.A. or Chicago living in coal sheds and working three jobs, hoping one day to buy a fixer-upper shotgun house at the foot of the mountains for under fifteen grand. There were long-haired carpenters taking accordion lessons from eighty-year-old Croatian miners. And in every place, an endless string of guitar players, just short of broke, sang in pine-paneled bars about rivers and snowstorms and cigarettes.

Most of the newcomers hung out for a summer or two and then moved on; others kept meaning to leave, but never did. They'd be all ready to go, and then summer would come on—unbridling the mountains and rivers, tossing the world with wildflowers. And pretty soon they'd fallen right back in love again, with all thoughts of leaving slipping away.

In the end, of course, most everyone moved on—going off to be lawyers or computer programmers or carpenters or teachers.

Jane and I closed the screen door on that little shack on the Salmon River in the spring of 1981. We left in the face of big changes in the country at large. By then, Joni Mitchell's "Big Yellow Taxi" had disappeared with her old man down some dark alley, yielding the stage to an appliance repairman's wet dream about making money for nothin' and getting chicks for free. Over in the Cineplex, the cameras had abandoned East Sixty-sixth Street in Manhattan, where they'd once fawned over those earnest neurotics of Annie Hall, instead moving south, to Wall Street, where Gordon Gekko reassured us that greed was good, that greed would save the country. The simple thoughts Jane and I had in our late teens, figuring boomers would keep reaching out, keep making connections, keep leaping and then looking for nets, seemed awfully naive. But we carried on, blowing new fires from the embers that nature had ignited years before.

* * * *

KENNETH REXROTH WAS FOND OF TELLING A TALE FROM childhood, when he befriended a ninety-year-old Native American man named Billy Sunlight, living in a chicken coop at the edge of a woodlot near Rexroth's grandmother's home on the Elkhart River. The old man took a shine to the boy, guiding him on outings to watch otters swimming in the river, gathering herbs, teaching him the Potawatomie names of animals and birds and woodland flowers. One day he came calling on Billy, only to open the door to his chicken coop and find the old man dead in his bunk, his hands crossed over his chest and a "luminous" look on his face. Rexroth later wrote that he wasn't afraid, that Billy had talked about his death with him, and it seemed just as it should be. Even so, as the weeks and months went by, sometimes Rexroth got terribly lonely, ended up crying for his old friend. "But not because he was dead, really. Only because he was gone from me and from the woods we loved."

He was about seven then—a boy who'd lost a summer friend, one who'd made it all the way to ninety. I was a middle-aged man, one who'd lost my wife and best friend of twenty-five years to a cold, dark river not two weeks past her fiftieth birthday. And yet from where I stand now, the difference seems one of degree. For me, as for that little boy, the lingering nut of the ache was in the fact that she was gone not just from me, but from the wild country we came to love.

My redemption would come in the form of a last request Jane had made years before, asking me if she died, to scatter her ashes in her five favorite wilderness areas. And so I did. Five treks to five unshackled landscapes. At first, the journeys broke my heart. Later they helped me piece it together again. In the end these trips would bring me back to nature again, to wilderness. To the lilting beauty of unkempt places—places powerful enough to woo the hearts not only of the young but of anyone willing to put down the search for meaning for a little while and just float in the sensations of being alive.

* * * *

YET AS I STAGGERED BACK TO LIFE AGAIN, DOING SO IN CLUMSY fits and starts, I found something unsettling—something I hadn't counted on: another kind of sorrow, a cultural one, a steady seep of loss and anger spreading across the northern Rockies. Several hours west of my home, people in the little town of Libby, Montana, were dying by the dozens from asbestos poisoning, courtesy of a vermiculite mine hosted by that pillar of corporate bad behavior, W.R. Grace. What had been just another quaint blue-collar mountain town was, a year after Jane's death, being called the deadliest Superfund site in America. Not a church service or wedding or family reunion happened in Libby that didn't include a heart-wrenching parade of winded men and women dragging IV hangers and oxygen bottles up and down the aisles.

Elsewhere, a fresh pack of angry white men were kicking off a new crusade against the federal government—against the national parks and forests, against too many goddamned regulations. And always, without fail, against wolves. Wolves as the "Bin Laden of the animal world," and as "God's great mistake." Pickup trucks from the Snake River to the North Dakota line sped down the highways with a fresh plaster of bumper stickers: "Wolves: Canadian Terrorists," and "Wolves: Smoke a Pack a Day."

Local newspapers carried photos of proud, grinning men with dead wolves hoisted in their arms, many having run the animals to exhaustion across twenty or thirty miles with snow machines, then pulling alongside to put a bullet in their heaving bodies. The grins never seemed so much about accomplishment, what with such kills taking about as much skill as hitting a deer with a car. The looks seemed more about release. That long-prized, almost impenetrable American fantasy of the rugged individual—long a theme song here—seemed to be dying out.

People from other places had the audacity to point out that, per capita, the West was receiving more federal dollars in subsidies than anywhere else in the country—for everything from agriculture to energy to timber production. Various groups were lining up to demand their public lands be managed not just for grazing and mining, but for recreation and wildlife. Meanwhile local paychecks were being rerouted through service industries— economies serving not just tourists, but retirees and second-home owners, the latter moving in with no particular allegiance to the rugged individualism that defined the code of the West. For many of the old guard, killing a wolf, especially a government wolf, was a shot glass of power in a river of gloom.

Outside the region, the news wasn't much better. Ice in the Arctic was melting faster than anyone had predicted. Wildfires were raging. In the year Jane died, some 5 million acres burned in Alaska alone; the following year, 3.7 million acres of Texas went up in smoke. Charges were leveled at the Bush administration for censoring government climate scientists, including the director of NASA's Goddard Institute for Space Studies, whose research showed striking connections between global warming and hurricane intensity.

Of course such problems weren't really new. But what made them harder to swallow was the fact that in my own generation especially, we seemed to be meeting them with less mettle, less audacity than we'd once laid claim to. The injustices we'd tried to face down when we were young, including giving good weight to matters of the earth, had wound down to little more than a wheezing sadness about how overwhelming it all was. Important issues like climate change were being tossed in the closet, stuffed into a box marked *things too hard to bear.* As if we'd traded away our spectacular naivety about changing the world for something smaller, safer, poorer.

In the wake of Jane's death, my reactions were probably more prickly than usual. I'd just lost the person most precious to me. To watch people selling the wolf as the devil, to hear others barking about how people shouldn't bitch about a little poison if it comes with a paycheck—all of it felt like a slight to life itself.

I ended up stuck off and on for years in that murky underworld of rage and blow. Only slowly, and with no end of stumbling, did I finally start embracing another truth. A truth that arose from the simple, unassailable fact that there are right now a fair number of people out there still trying to live as if the planet mattered. Indigenous people—more powerful today than they've been in years—are pushing sovereignty in a heroic effort to protect the air and water of tribal lands, steering toward a future that many of the rest of us still lack the courage to even imagine. At the same time, men and women in dozens of countries, from every walk of life—and of all ages, though a great many are young—are discovering yet again that a relationship with nature is one way to a riper, more expanded sense of life. They're stewards of bigheartedness. Their efforts are tonic for sorrowful times.

If such paths are difficult, and they always are, they can at least be said to offer unspeakable tenderness, astonishing beauty. Just like the path Jane and I set out on more than thirty years ago, when we headed off in Rexroth's footsteps, out onto open land, heads up and looking—looking at everything—angling for some new way of dreaming up the world.

TOWARD A SETTING SUN

S omewhere on the far side of Winnipeg, in a town I haven't
so much forgotten as never knew, Martha pulls the van
to the curb, gets out without a word, crosses the street into
some stranger's yard, and starts pilfering flowers. I sit in the
passenger seat with my broken leg jammed against the windshield, craning my neck to look up and down the neat rows
of little boxy houses, white and blue and pink, half expecting
some little old lady to fling open the screen door and loose a
pair of schnauzers on her. But soon she's back, climbing behind
the wheel to lay a fistful of lilac and pear blossoms on the dashboard, nesting them against the cardboard box that holds the

ashes. A hundred or so miles down the road, as the flowers begin to pale, we slow down, lower the windows, and with no small feeling of ceremony cast them to the prairie. Then another stop in some other little farm town to swipe more flowers. So it goes, two thousand miles across the north country. A sluggish, one-car memorial procession and petty crime spree, from Mr. Blake's funeral home on Fourth Street in Thunder Bay, home again, to the faraway uplands of Montana.

* * * *

IT'S TAKEN THE BETTER PART OF A DAY TO GET TO THE Canadian prairie—that hazy line of longitude where seven hundred miles of balsam and birch finally begin to yield, replaced by roadsides of bluestem and wild rye. Out beyond the loose scatter of towns this is lonely country—wind and sky and fruitless thoughts. I recall years ago being near here on an even smaller road, tucked tight against the highline of North Dakota; through the windshields of cars going in the other direction were lone drivers with newspapers propped against the steering wheels, reading. This is that kind of place. The sort of landscape that makes people edgy, their patience finally failing against these plates of sky, these endless oceans of wheat.

It's been four days since I lost my wife. Since then, the whole region has descended into raucous, lumbering rain. Water fills the potholes and hollows on dirt roads adjacent to the highway, lies in the parking lots of grocery stores and across the bays of gas stations, churned to ripples by a relentless wind. In the ditches along the roads, the grass and sunflowers have come on so fast that mowing crews can't keep up with them. It leaves the two-lane we're traveling—already a miracle of understatement—looking tenuous, like something from the '60s, when a long drive on an open highway seemed like some sort of escapade.

An hour from the border, Martha wipes her eyes and straightens in the seat—startles me with a smack of her palm against the steering wheel.

"We've gotta get some carrot juice," she sniffs. "The border's coming. Carrots'll ground us."

I applaud the idea, however strange. Out here on the prairie, though, we might as well be digging for truffles. At one point we spend ten minutes leafing through phone books looking for a health-food store, finding nothing, until finally it dawns on us that we could get all the benefits of carrot juice simply by eating carrots. A few miles up the road, I spot a produce sign at the lone business in the town of Elm Creek, a gas station and quick stop, and I hobble inside to find a single rotting bunch of celery and seven apples. The owner is a bulky man, smiling from under a blond mustache as he hauls baskets of chicken parts from a vat of hot oil. When I ask about carrots, he gets a concerned look—not so much like he thinks I'm nuts, but as if he can sense the depth of my troubles. Without a word he goes back into his apartment, pulls a bag of carrots from his own refrigerator, sells it for almost nothing.

"Good luck," he calls out after me.

So we roll out of Canada with wilting flowers on the dashboard and mealy pieces of carrot between our teeth. On hearing of the accident, the border patrolman stumbles, goes on to tell us how some friends were trying to get him to take a rafting trip on the Russian River in California but water scares him and he's nervous about the whole idea. He stops short, blinks—as if suddenly realizing he's blathering. Then he's back to business, taking a haphazard look around the inside of the van, opening a box or two. Clearly relieved, he waves us on, arm outstretched, a lone finger pointing toward the empty fields of North Dakota.

From here nearly to home the roads are mapped precisely to the cardinal points of a compass. Strung first with little wheat towns, then, as we move farther west, with little Hereford and Angus towns. In every community flags are waving, proud even as plywood boards are being screwed across the windows of the downtown storefronts. Over the past decade, the region has lost thousands of residents, some areas now claiming fewer people than 175 years ago, in the glory days of the Sioux. Beyond the open windows we catch fluty snippets of meadowlark from random fence posts—and from wet ditches, the whir and twitter of red-winged blackbirds, hanging sideways from cattails and swaying in the wind.

My doctors in Thunder Bay were troubled when I said I was going home by road, worried I might develop blood clots. With that in mind I mostly ride shotgun, perched in a captain's chair with my broken leg propped up and pointed down the highway. Still, every few hours, I tell Martha I want to trade off, yank the leg down and hobble around to the other side, crawl in, and drive for a hundred miles or so with my left foot. Friends who hear I've been behind the wheel will cast dubious looks at Martha, as if as a guardian she leaves something to be desired.

"I never got the sense it was up for discussion," she'll tell them.

In truth this westward journey is the only obsession left for me. A forlorn mission to carry home that box on the dashboard, at a pace no faster than a '79 Chevy van can manage against a prairie wind.

* * * *

EVER SINCE THE HIGHWAY OPENED UP, I CAN'T STOP FIDDLING with the tape deck—fast-forward and then rewind, a little more then a little less, playing one song and then yanking the tape to find another. Intentionally picking music that stabs me in the heart. First it's Bonnie Raitt, in a sort of aw-shucks version of "Your Sweet and Shiny Eyes," a song that recalls two old friends down on the Mexican border clanking glasses to one of their birthdays, drinking salty margaritas with a stranger named Fernando. For twenty years Jane and I played that song to each other on every birthday—including two weeks ago, on her fiftieth, rolling down U.S. 2 through the jack pines of northern Michigan. "Young and wild," croons Bonnie as the blue flax rolls by, "we drove 900 miles of Texas highway, to the Mexican border, as the day was comin' on."

Another tank of gas in Carlyle, then Kate Wolf: "I've been

walkin' in my sleep, countin' troubles 'stead of countin' sheep."
And on Highway 12, within a stone's throw of the Montana line,
Jackson Browne, "Running on Empty."

Now and then I turn to stare over my left shoulder, above
a small counter in the center of the van, to a cork bulletin board
crowded with faded photographs: The two of us clutching a
bottle of champagne on the Lochsa River in northern Idaho
at the end of two thousand miles of trail. Thanksgiving in the
Chisos Mountains of West Texas. Three shots of Abby the traveling cat. Another of us in late August on the rounded shoulders of the Berkshires, all soft and green and sweating in the
summer sun.

Beside the photos is a wire basket holding one of the journals
Jane kept filled with notes from our research trips: Trail descriptions. Perfect campsites. Random thoughts from late in the
evening, parked out in the woods somewhere, halfway through
our second beer. Notes from the redwoods and Point Reyes in
California, from Padre Island in southern Texas, the dark hills
of North Carolina, the Chiricahua Mountains of Arizona. From
the Dakota Badlands and Florida's Juniper River. Notes from the
Utah desert, when the big blue van gained air during a heroic,
ill-fated attempt to cross a washed-out arroyo after a rainstorm.
From times spent poking along Edward Abbey's favorite jeep
roads in West Texas. From a cowboy line camp in northern
Arizona. Squatting in the sand on a beach in Mexico. And of
course notes from the Rockies, up and down that particular spill
of mountains too many times to count.

She was five foot five with straight brown hair, managing to always seem younger than her age in part by the enthusiasm of her smile. Much like her father, a salt-of-the-earth seed corn farmer from Indiana, walking down the street she made it a point to engage the gaze of strangers, believing it good to make connections even when it probably wasn't. Her laugh was sudden, a little rowdy, the first note exploding in a spurt of holler followed by a quick hand to her mouth, as if she was as surprised as anyone by such outbursts. Most days she rose at the crack of dawn with the trace of a grin already showing at the corners of her mouth.

She'd been an outdoor educator her entire adult life, working from the canyons of the Southwest, north to Yellowstone; in her off-hours she wrote letters to family, called from pay phones the people we knew just to say hi, did aerobics in the living room with Jane Fonda while the snow fell, made cookies and gave most of them away. She performed magic tricks for small kids—mostly tricks her dad taught her—and if anyone in her audience was so inclined, she was happy to go jump into piles of leaves or build snow forts in somebody's backyard or roll down some grassy hill for the sole purpose of getting dizzy.

We'd been restless children, destined to become restless adults. Proud members of the last generation to soothe the angst of youth not with Ritalin, but with road trips. What started with the Beats of the '40s and '50s—twenty-somethings from the Midwest and East Coast, pushing west in Ramblers and Roadmasters, Nomads and Bel Airs—ended with quixotic Pollyannas like us, westering in Volkswagens and Impalas and

Ford Econolines. Long before I could even drive, I lay in my bed on spring nights in South Bend, Indiana, listening to the groan of freight trains two blocks away, rumbling west toward Chicago on the Grand Trunk line, wanting nothing more than to go. At seventeen I made it, hopping into those boxcars on Friday and Saturday nights, rolling away past crumbling brick warehouses that circled the edges of the city out into a land of fields and woodlots and pot-holed county roads leading to who knows where.

Jane too started young, making tents out of bedsheets at the edges of her family's cornfields. Sweating through the firefly summers, lulled to sleep by the smell of dirt, thrilled, she once told me, by the fact that from the middle of July all the way to harvest, those sprawling cornfields held at least a modest chance to leave the known world. Disappear. Get lost. Nine months after we met, each of us sold our cars and on a cold December day laid down the money for the slightly used blue Chevy van Martha and I are riding in now, having found it on a car lot in the tiny town of Syracuse, Indiana. With my father's help, through five months of sanding and sawing and nailing and wiring, we turned it into a sixteen-foot rolling home called Moby. In the spring of 1980 we busted a bottle of cheap champagne across the front bumper, then pushed out of the heartland on a journey stretching across twenty-five years and some 350,000 miles.

* * * *

TEN DAYS AGO, DRIVING THROUGH THE OUTSKIRTS OF
Sudbury, Ontario, Jane turned to me, and in the first such conversation we'd had in more than a decade, asked if I remembered how if something ever happened to her, she wanted her
ashes scattered in her favorite places. Five of them in all, from
the red rock of southern Utah to the foothills of Wyoming's
Absaroka Range; from the granite domes of central Idaho to
the Beartooths of south-central Montana, to a certain high valley in northeast Yellowstone.

Of course I remember, I told her.

Now, wrapped in this impossible fog of grief, I have only one
thought about the future: That after my leg heals, when neighbors are no longer bringing over covered dishes, when friends are
no longer stopping by to mow my lawn and vacuum my house,
no longer driving me to the mountains so I can sleep under the
stars—probably sometime in early fall—I'll make up the bed
in the back of the van, stock the tiny fridge, pick just the right
music, and drive away. Beside me will be a jar, a beautiful jar.
One last time for the two of us, outward bound, into the West.

THE RELICS OF HOME

As best I recall, I started leaving the ordinary around age seven, escaping by ascension—going up twelve feet, sometimes fifteen—sitting in the crook of maples or oaks and hugging the trunks, curtains of big green leaves wound up in the wind, making noises like rivers running through the sky. Kid-style adventure, mostly. But on some days—days when my mother's rage was running, when she'd been at me with that studded belt she kept hung behind the bedroom door, spinning me around until my bare butt and thighs were covered in a splatter of welts—on those days, the trees were sanctuary. On those days, I'd squirm higher still, to the uppermost branches big enough to hold my weight. And I'd sit there, sometimes for an hour or more, way above everything, halfway to the sky.

At about the same time, Jane was doing her own version of leaving the ordinary, mostly in a loose toss of woods at the edge of her family's farm. A modest patch of mild disorder where foxes did half gainers through the air, landing with front paws pinned to unsuspecting mice and voles. Where raccoons waddled up to the creek and washed their faces—looking, she said, like overfed hoodlums cleaning up after a hard night of stealing. In time those encounters led her to join the Girl Scouts, and later to take a job as a counselor at the Kentuckiana Girl Scout Camp in northern Kentucky. Nicknamed Calamity Jane, she kept the sash from her uniform hung in our closet for years, festooned with twenty embroidered merit badges: among them "Outdoor Cook," "Drawing and Painting," "First Aid," "Reader," "World Knowledge," and "Adventurer." I always thought it strange there was no "Rambler" badge, though for all her urge to wander, her chance wouldn't come until later, long after the uniforms had been put away.

It was the best of luck for us to have come under the spell of trees and foxes and hedgerows at a time when millions of other Americans were falling in love with nature, too—in city parks and urban wetlands, along the Appalachian Trail, the California redwoods, at Yellowstone and Yosemite, Rocky Mountain and Great Smoky Mountains and Acadia national parks. Mostly the travelers were young, not ten years older than us, keen to be slipping into that now and then silly, now and then profound attraction that rolls across this country every forty or fifty years. A drive not unrelated to one that exploded in America in the 1780s. And again in the 1830s. And again in the 1870s. Then still again in the first two decades of the twentieth century—a time so full of fire that journalists described it as a movement like no other in the world. A time when the best-selling books were nature books. When naturalists like John Burroughs and Ernest Thompson Seton were rock stars.

In 1913, a pot-bellied, beer-swigging part-time illustrator from New England named Joe Knowles sidled up to his friends in a Boston bar and ordered up pints. As usual, they joked, ribbed one another. Argued politics. But eventually the talk drifted to nature, to wilderness. And that was hardly unusual for the times. Any American over thirty had memories of the official closing of the frontier—the frontier being defined as a line "out west," beyond which population densities were less than two people per square mile. For a nation long convinced that its best qualities had arisen from life along that shifting line, such a closing was a big deal. Indeed, for decades afterward, people debated and generally worried about the effects of that milestone on everything from individual character to national identity.

Beyond that, those same years saw no end of outrage against the unbridled pillaging of nature by the robber barons. And also against the fact that young boys and girls who'd been raised on farms were working seventy-hour weeks in the mills, some dying in fires, others crippled by lung disease. Senator William Borah, of Idaho, introduced a bill to oversee general health conditions for working kids, asking the government to do for them what it'd done long before for calves and pigs.

And all that fed into that scene in that Boston bar, when late in the evening after God knows how much beer, Joe Knowles stood up and puffed out his chest.

"I've half a mind to strip naked and run off into the woods for two or three months, live as a wild man. Just to prove Americans still have sap in their veins."

Everyone was impressed. The next morning, a Boston reporter named Michael McCeough knocked on Joe's door, probably rousing him from a hangover.

"Remember that thing you said last night?" asked McCeough. "The thing about running off naked to live as a wild man?"

Who knows if Knowles recalled. But he was a proud man.

"Well," the reporter went on, "my editor thinks it'd be a great circulation gimmick. We'd like to sponsor you."

Which is how in August 1913, on the far shore of King and Bartlett Lake in western Maine, it came to pass that Joe Knowles stood in a light drizzle wearing something like a G-string, explaining the mission to a bewildered group of reporters, telling them about the need for us all to remember we still have sap in our veins. The idea, he went on, had come from a dream he'd had of being lost in the woods, alone and naked, with little hope of getting out.

"Not much of a dream. But a damn real one."

It would be one of the greatest publicity stunts of all time. Knowles emerged from the woods two months later a full-blown hero—not just in New England, but coast to coast. A book of his adventures sold more than 250,000 copies. On emerging from the woods, some twenty thousand people turned out to see him, including thousands on the Boston Common alone. The chief physician at Harvard pronounced him to be the fittest human specimen he'd ever seen. He went on to tour vaudeville for two and a half years with top billing.

"Behold a sermon two months long for the people of the United States!" cried Herbert Johnson, celebrated pastor of Boston's Warren Avenue Church, shortly after Knowles stumbled out of the woods. Pastor Johnson went on to say how he wished those who worshipped gold could understand the underlying spirit of the wilderness, that what Knowles did would make men and women across the country go into the woods. And in the woods they would stop and think. And the more they thought, the longer the flag would wave.

The boomers who ended up carrying that same water, refloating yet another round of slightly wacky, American-style craving for nature in the 1960s and '70s, were by sheer numbers a force to reckon with. And their quick, big embrace of the last untrammeled places was for Jane and me a fine alternative to the straight roads of Indiana—the straight lawns and straight furrows of corn, the straight lines of kids waiting outside the schoolhouse door. It's true that by the time we hit our teen years, Indiana was already lidded and torn. But here and there, even in the Hoosier state, there were enough pieces left for us to feel like part of the movement, the celebration. What was left of those unkempt lands felt to us a lot like the way Thomas Wolfe described nature: places where miracles not only happen, but where they happen all the time. Bees still hovered over sky-blue flax blossoms, then flew away to points unknown. Lightning bugs lit up the summer nights. Cardinals appeared blood red against the snow, magically plucking out tiny seeds hidden deep inside the drifts.

* * * *

THE OLD CHEVY VAN CAME TO REST IN EARLY JUNE, PARKED beside the house in the gravel driveway, under the branches of a towering Douglas fir. I sat outside, crumpled in a plastic lawn chair, my broken leg on a lodgepole stump while my friend John unloaded the van, carrying to the garage bits and pieces of our ill-fated journey. At one point he stopped and sighed, squatted down and told me I didn't have to thank him every time he gathered up another load. Abby the traveling cat, eighteen at the time, as well as a younger gray tabby named Ruby knew something wasn't right. Normally off messing around in the woods, they wouldn't leave my side—waiting and watching under my chair, trading off lying against my stomach. Nervously watching as John pulled out yellow and green river bags, a pair of canoe paddles, lifejackets, maps, nature guides, rain gear. A torn, tattered black and blue wet suit the paramedics had cut off me after my rescue.

The early months after my return—June through August, which in the Rockies are almost always brilliant—were in the year 2005 filled with cold and bluster and rain. Things were being over-watered, growing through the early weeks of the season not gently, as usually happens, but in tangles, heavy snarls of fescue and bluebells and saplings. "Stupidly fertile," as author Rinda West once put it. One day midsummer, desperate for elbow room, for a sense of order, I tied my gas-powered Weed Eater onto one of my crutches with a short length of cotton rope then stumbled out to the edges of the yard and started cutting back the bluestem and Oregon grape, the low-lying shrubs. It wasn't pretty: lurching forward a step with the crutches clenched under my armpits, swinging the machine in a wide arc in front of me, stopping there long enough to cut what I could reach, then moving on. A close friend overheard someone talking about my psychotic yard work and phoned for an explanation. "Oh, *crutch!*" she said after I started to explain. "The way I heard it, you'd tied a Weed Eater to your *crotch.*"

We were together in these aspen woods, on this creek, for more than fourteen years. We knew the moose that ate the landscaping, and the black bear that liked to saunter across the deck and stare at us through the bedroom window, painting the glass with slobber. The ferocious little mink, too, scurrying up and down the island every June with a bad case of the munchies. We could show you the fallen trees where male grouse drummed, calling for mates. Tell you which of the ice bridges whitetail deer used to cross the creek in the heart of winter, predict the days in March when the Canada geese would return, dropping out of sheets of snow.

We could mosey with you through the aspen to where the tipi stood, recounting what it sounded like from the inside on summer nights, when rain drummed against the canvas. Point to the place on the deck where in warm months we laid out the mattress from the van, drifting off to sleep to the sounds of the creek pushing north to the Yellowstone River, and every now and then, to hollow strains of great horned owls calling from the cottonwoods.

We knew the stages by which pockets of forest turned gold in the fall, the places where buttercups first opened in the spring. We could point to a line of grass-covered notches on the east horizon, marking where the sun rose in any given month. Show you the path of the moon across the winter sky.

The house itself had been a kind of fruiting of our relationship. Designed long before we even owned property, the rooms appeared in various daydreams while living on the road for seven months in the van, part of a rambling pair of writing projects in the Pacific Northwest. One morning over breakfast in a café in Lincoln, Montana, Jane plucked a white napkin from the stainless spenser sitting on the Formica table, spread it open halfway, fished a stubby pencil out of her day pack.

"What room should we start with?"

"I'm thinking kitchen," I said, eyeing the room full of ranchers and loggers drinking coffee and eating buttermilk pancakes, trying to imagine the right size. "Not too big. But big enough for people to hang out."

"Done!" Then she drew another, smaller rectangle on the

napkin. "I'd like a place for a washer and dryer. Maybe a laundry tub. With dried plants hanging from the ceiling."

On it went through the good months of summer, the drawing expanding with the passing days. We talked of an east-facing window in the bedroom to let in morning light. A garage for the van. Parked deep in the forest at the end of the day, she'd carefully unfold the napkin in the last of the light, study it without a word for twenty or thirty minutes, then refold it, pressing it like a flower between the pages of the road notes.

"It'll be good for us to have a home base," she liked to say. For all her love of wandering she was keen on being anchored to a place—not so much for comfort, but for a certain common sense she found in the rooms and the yards and the main streets that scribed her life.

In the wake of her death, friends dropped by to pay their respects, bringing soups and pastas and casseroles and salads and cakes. Some walked through the house and caught their breath, as if seized by the thought that these very things—the wall hangings and photos on the old piano, the dried plants that did in fact end up hanging from the logs in the laundry room, just as she imagined—had in the blink of an eye become prompts for grief. They laid their offerings on the counter and hugged me. We'd cry for a minute or two. Then they'd let themselves out and drive away.

And I'd go back to the photos—spilling out of bowls and baskets, some held on the refrigerator door by little fruit-shaped magnets, others in frames, hung on the walls of the living room and bedroom and bathroom and hallway. One in particular, taped to the side of a metal filing cabinet in her office, I went back to over and over again: a shot of her on a swing I'd made for her birthday out of a slab of barn wood, which with a little reckless behavior I managed to fasten to the high branches of a cottonwood tree outside the back door with forty-foot lengths of rope. In the photo she's wearing brown pants and a long-sleeved shirt the color of spring sky, caught swooping past the camera on her way to the edge of the creek bank, legs out straight and leaning backward from the waist, grinning at the camera. Swinging the way self-assured little girls swing on warm mornings before the start of school. Of the various gifts I gave her over the years—flowers for anniversaries, the skis and backpacks and other outdoor gear she always wanted for Christmas—that swing, which she'd asked for on her forty-eighth birthday, made her especially happy.

The next morning I rose to find her at the window, looking out at the swing being pushed through a graceful sweep by a steady breeze.

"Look! It even works without us."

"The world's first perpetual-motion swing," I suggested.

She nodded, then pointed at Abby the traveling cat, sitting at the edge of the woods in front of the swing, her head rolling back and forth with the movement of the ropes.

"And a giant cat toy."

The previous year, she'd worked her last season as a ranger in Yellowstone, the end of seven years teaching at the park's brilliant nature school for junior high kids, ending what was probably the best job of her life for the chance to spend time closer to home. She was apprehensive about leaving, troubled by the hole in her life she knew would be there when she was no longer teaching. Still, in the photo, she's wearing the giddy, slightly silly look she could muster even in the face of worry. As if putting on the look of happy took her halfway to being there.

There were other mementos in the house, of course—mostly bits of nature gathered from other places: baskets filled with pinecones—Digger and Coulter plucked from trails in the Sierras, lodgepole and ponderosa and whitebark from the Rockies, jack and eastern white pine from New Hampshire. Her climbing harness dangled from a hook in the corner of her office, above a small table set with binoculars, field guides, a small hand lens. And beside the table was a stack of homemade plant presses, each fashioned from two pieces of fiberboard filled with sheets of newspaper and bound tight with pack straps, used across years of research we did for a series of nature guides. One morning after returning from Canada, I unclipped the straps and leafed through the layers of newspaper, finding marsh fern fronds from Pennsylvania and wiregrass from Wyoming; red fir branches from the northern Sierras, golden heather from the coast of Maine. And in the middle of the press, a pair of may-flowers from New England, their ivory blooms faded now to a ghostly, translucent pale.

The mayflowers had come from a deep woodland in western Connecticut, the one journey we ever made where her boundless enthusiasm proved unfortunate. She'd been out faithfully keying plants, when all of a sudden she spotted in the distance an elderly man bending down under a cluster of beech trees. He too, evidently, was taking pleasure in some exquisite patch of blooms—a last show of wildflowers before the killing frost. Hurrying over to share in the find, she suddenly stopped in her tracks, having discovered the guy not studying plants at all, but partially disrobed, squatting over a freshly dug hole trying to do his business. "Guess you caught me with my pants down," he offered sheepishly. She muttered a fast apology and scurried away.

These remnants, the flowers and pinecones and photographs and binoculars and dog-eared field guides, were the trappings of life lived as though nature were both wings and nest. Touchstones to places where wounds got tended. Juniper berries from southern Utah, gathered during a sad, weeklong meander following my father's sudden death. White quartz from Montana's Line Creek Plateau, found after a hard trip to Indiana, when we'd sat with Jane's mother in the Alzheimer's ward and held her hand and told her all manner of news we knew she didn't understand, fed her and rubbed lotion on the dry places of her face, then kissed her cheek and gone away.

* * * *

SEVERAL MONTHS AFTER JANE'S DEATH ON THE KOPKA, sorting through remnants of her life, I stumbled across a box of letters she'd written to my mother. Most held the usual chatty news—birthday wishes, notes from some adventure. One of them, though, written in the fall of 1982, slammed the breath right out of me.

"One of my biggest fears," she'd written, "is to drown in murky water—in a place where you can't see the bottom."

Which was an exact description of the Kopka River, stained the color of weak tea by tannins leached from the spruce forest. I struggled for days after that, thinking all over again how we could've just as easily gone backpacking. Taken a bike trip. Stayed at home and laid in the hammock and read books and drunk margaritas. Cleaned the fucking garage.

There's this obscure rule in science, in physics, called deterministic chaos. Look it up in a college textbook and you might find this example: Toss a leaf into a stream at the head of a current and see where it comes out at the end of the flow. Place another leaf in the exact same location, oriented precisely the same way, and because of tiny chaotic forces beyond our ability to measure, it will come out at the bottom of the current somewhere else entirely.

If we hadn't stopped at that canoe shop so Jane could buy me that new flotation bag for my birthday, we would've headed home to Montana without ever hearing of the Kopka River. If we'd slept another ten minutes before departing. If we'd been in a boat a foot longer or a foot shorter. If at the head of the rapid the canoe had been one foot, one inch over to the left or right. If I'd given a somewhat lighter or harder draw stroke . . . Then maybe she would've lived, would've kept from hitting her head and being knocked unconscious when the boat finally flipped, pitching us into that screaming water.

It was a fixation that pushed me close as I've ever come to losing my mind. Late in the evening, when the last of the alpenglow was fading above the conifer ridges of Towne Mountain, I was often on the edge of panic. One dark night in early July, hyperventilating, I called my friend Mark, and he hustled over in his black Toyota truck to sit across from me in the living room while I muttered and clutched my chest. "She always said when it came her time to go," I told him again, "she wanted to be in the wilds, doing what she loved." And also, about how less than a minute before the wreck, two loons—among her favorite creatures—swam up to the canoe on a lake dappled with sunlight, and she laid her paddle on her lap and looked up at the sky, shouting what were very nearly her last words:

"Thank you, Universe!"

I told him there should be some comfort in that. And one more time, right on cue, he nodded as if it were true.

WATER TO STONE, ONE

I t was hard for us to keep up with all the ways the boomers were hugging the remote corners of the American wild. By ski and backpack, horse and raft and mountain bike, in harness on the faces of mountains, dangling from climbing ropes. And while we tried most all of it, canoeing had a special place in our hearts. It was a good-sense way of traveling in the American West, a region where everything kneels at the river: elk and deer and grizzly and eagle and osprey, raccoon and wolverine and mountain lion, kingfishers and dippers and giant rafts of chattering ducks and geese. To be quietly afloat was to brush against secrets, where you saw things other creatures never meant for you to see.

When we were backpacking, we were two people sharing a single journey. But in a canoe, we danced: the person in the back of the boat setting the general course, the one in the front refining it, especially in whitewater, cueing the rear paddler to obstacles by her choice of draw stroke or sweep or pry. Early in our marriage we'd been to Audubon Camp of the West outside Dubois, Wyoming; one evening, we saw a couple in their eighties canoeing down the Wind River. Their paddling was magic, as graceful and efficient as humans are allowed to be, getting down the river with almost no strokes at all. Only occasionally would the old man's wooden paddle flash in the stern—a slight, quick movement at just the right moment, matched exactly to the choices made by the old woman sitting in the bow. Jane and I turned to each other and smiled. We wanted to be like them some day.

* * * *

THE TRIP ON THE KOPKA WAS SUPPOSED TO BE A FLOAT IN THE park. Two hours paddling through easy Class II rapids and across two lakes, broken by one long portage around an unrunnable stretch of whitewater. We were playful, picking hard routes. The sun blinked in and out of clouds heavy with rain, casting long shafts of spring light.

It was three weeks before our twenty-fifth anniversary. On the flat water of Kopka Lake, with paddles rising and falling, we told each other how good it had been.

"Another twenty-five?" I called out from the stern of the boat.

Jane twisted her head to the side so I could hear better. "Why not!"

Two days earlier, we'd finished five generous days at a renowned paddling school in eastern Ontario, where students came from all over North America to hang out with some of the best kayakers and canoeists on the continent. When the course ended, the instructors passed out handwritten evaluations, ours coming from a hearty twenty-five-year-old named Judy. Jane was eager to read it, pulling it from the envelope before we were even out of the parking lot. It began with a personal note:

> *I think I'd first like to comment on your communication. It was amazing. I've never seen a couple work through the tricky moments as smoothly as you two. You guys have taught me what I'd like my communication to be like in a long-term tandem relationship. As I truly believe strong communication is integral to tandem paddlers, you two have a very solid base for all paddling adventures.*

Four hours after reading Judy's comments, on the outskirts of Algonquin Park, Jane read them out loud again. She did the same thing the next morning, outside Sudbury. Like she found Judy's comments reassuring, a portent of all the good things still to come. There'd been times at that paddling school when we were really in the sweet spot—lit up by this sense of clasping hands with the river, holding not too tight, not too loose.

That morning, when we finally got across Kopka Lake and reached the portage pullout, the trail was blocked by a chest-high jumble of blown-down timber, the result of a massive ice storm three years earlier. We scouted alternatives, in the end deciding we could safely take out closer to the head of the rapids.

When we got there in the boat, though, a strange hydraulic flow from near-record rains sucked us toward the teeth of the rapids. Unable to run for shore because of a fallen tree jutting from the bank into the river, in a matter of seconds we were in the thick of things, devoured by a fury of whitewater. On each side of the riverbank were dozens more fallen trees, half in and half out of the water. Known as "strainers," they're the kiss of disaster, routinely flipping boats and pinning paddlers against the underwater branches. Nor could we maneuver into eddies, calm pools formed on the downstream side of large rocks. High water had obliterated all trace of them.

Waves of cold water crashed over the bow, soaking Jane, leaving gallon after gallon in the bottom of the boat. For that reason alone—sixty pounds of water, then eighty, then a hundred pounds, sloshing and rocking the canoe and exposing the gunnels to the river—we knew there'd be no getting through. Still, we were on our knees, paddling with everything. I took my cues from Jane, watching as she cut hard draw strokes on the right side of the boat and then crossed to draw on the other side, here and there a desperate pry—everything to keep us from hurtling into some toothy lump of granite I couldn't even see. But by then the boat was too heavy, impossible to steer.

We made it about 100 yards.

The end came at the top of a rock-strewn cascade. When the boat finally rolled, I spent the first ten seconds under water, freeing myself from the Velcro straps we used for stability when paddling on our knees. I could hear the grinding and thudding of the canoe as it slammed into one rock then another—sounds I can still hear to this day, booming in my ears in the middle of the night. Back up on the surface again, I got into swiftwater rescue position—butt up, feet forward, facing downstream—all to keep my feet from being snared in rock jumbles on the river-bed. I couldn't see Jane. But the water was incredibly heavy. She could've been five feet from me and I'd have never known it.

Like most whitewater boaters, I'd taken swims in rapids. But I'd never been so totally helpless. Out of control. Screaming curses as the river slammed me into boulders, tearing and pum-meling my backside. Even with a life jacket on, I was twice pinned to the bottom of recirculation pools, inhaling water, close to drowning. But then I made it out again, back into the roar. Near the end of the rapid, I catapulted over a four-foot waterfall, my right leg driving hard into a rock crevice, snapping like a twig. Coughed out at last into the quiet of a flush pond, I swam over to the canoe and clung to the side, stood on my good leg, and waited for Jane. Waited some more.

HUNGER SEASON

Our long dance with rivers had reached a high point five years earlier, in the so-called Barren Lands of the Canadian far north—twice the size of Texas, sprawling across half a million square miles, one of the biggest tracts of wilderness in the world. We'd first journeyed there in 2000, embarking by canoe with four friends along the Hood River, just inside the Arctic Circle. The floatplane touched down after three hours of northbound flight from Yellowknife; with the weather souring, we hustled to unload gear, then confirmed with the pilot a pickup sixteen days later, upstream from where the Hood makes a final exhale into the Arctic Sound. He was anxious to be off, drawing in the anchor lines from the floats, climbing into the cockpit. After taxiing back out into the lake, he took off with a roar, drawing a wide arc toward the south and finally fading from sight, then from sound, leaving us to the wind-shorn tundra. We didn't so much feel alone as vulnerable. That vulnerability, in turn, brought alertness. And just by being alert, we were able to catch a kid-sized feeling of having stumbled into Eden.

Jane and I stood together in that far country and watched gyrfalcons streak out of bony canyons; hiked tundra heaved by frost into mounds and hummocks; sat open-mouthed as caribou danced across the humped ground like trotter ponies on a groomed track. By day we drifted past musk oxen grunting over patches of sedge along the riverbanks, wolverines scuttling up the hills like angry little bears. Once, a pair of wolves appeared across the river, a white male and black female, playing with their pups so enthusiastically they sent thick clouds of dust drifting through the air. Then the adults spotted us and went into action, squirreling the young into a den. As we pushed off, the male trotted alongside on the top of a small ridge, howling, anxious for us to be away.

And then there was the light. Sun hovering above the treeless horizon even at midnight, as if stuck in flight, soaking the fireweed and tufts of cotton grass in dark honey. And of course there were mosquitoes, great clouds of them swarming every evening outside our screened-in dinner tent, hungry for a bite of these strange warm-bloods that chattered on past midnight, raising cups of whiskey and smoking foul-smelling cigars. Later on, in our sleeping tents, absent a hearty wind, the little blood-suckers careened into the nylon walls with the insistent patter of a good rain.

Late one afternoon after camp was set, out walking the tundra we spotted on a distant ridge a long line of piled rocks—so-called "stone men," erected centuries ago by indigenous people. Mistaking the rocks for humans, migrating caribou would avoid them, walking instead toward hunters lying in wait.

Without a word Jane and I sat down side by side, just staring at the stones. Trying to fathom what such lives were like. Imagining families, entire villages, moving by foot across hundreds of miles of tundra, shadowing the caribou herds—hop-scotching the rough ground with kids and babies in tow, steering around an endless reach of bogs and quags.

"There would've been few second chances," Jane finally said. "I wonder how that affects people—I mean, when they know how thin the thread is that keeps them alive."

I told her that having danger so close at hand, day after day, season after season, might make a person worry more.

"I don't know," she said. "With life and death in your face like that, maybe worry would seem useless. A silly indulgence."

Even in that great wild north country, one of the last great wildernesses in the world, we were aware during our visit that big changes were coming. An energy boom was on the horizon, with some forty thousand square miles already slated for drilling. Diamond mines, too, stoking what would soon become a frenzy of roads and bulldozers and sheet metal towns. For the time being, though, the land was still in control. The Inuit living here, who possess an untethered cosmology, believe there are no divine mother or father figures steering the cosmos. No gods of sun or wind or snow. Nor are there any eternal punishments in the hereafter, as there are no such punishments in the here and now. Life and prayer and dreams are calved from the sense that here, everything—from money to creed—is sooner or later broken by ice and swept to the sea. Their biggest priority is the present moment, focusing on it to a degree most of us would be hard-pressed to match. The essence of life, they say—the essential truths of the universe—is found not in some past glory, not in some future accomplishment, but right now, in experiencing a deep relationship with what's around us.

If only our generation could've kept looking, could've kept living a while longer with the questions. If we hadn't ended up frozen in notions of the outback formed the last time we imagined it, when its greatest value seemed to be as a testing ground for the muscle of youth. Not that Jane and I didn't see it that way, too. But early on, in the midst of some hard teen years, nature had also sparked in us the idea that we had some kind of place in the order of things. It kept us eager for moments having nothing to do with hustling cereal or soap or self-improvement, for that part of the world that never expected us to be anything but what we were, never encouraged us to ask for anything we didn't already have.

THE FIRST GOODBYE

Long ago, cartographers from the land of mental health erected signposts for journeys through the blackness of loss. *At least he's moved out of denial,* friends and family might have been saying to one another. Around the next bend would be anger. Then bargaining. Then the crumbling backstreets of depression. Finally would come a return home—an "acceptance"—at which point flowers would bloom again and light would shine in the windows. Whatever. In that first autumn, it made no more sense to hope for a normal life than it would for a man who's lost his leg to expect to wake up one morning and find a new one growing in its place.

It was barely past Labor Day when I decided to make the first scattering of Jane's ashes. That time of year when the coats of the whitetail deer are thickening, turning from the reddish brown of midsummer to the color of wet sand. The time of sandhill cranes gathering into small groups, chortling to one another about the old urge for going. That time when the color of the sky deepens from powder to cobalt blue. Free of the cast on my leg, I was desperate for movement, and the movement I wanted most was something having to do with honoring Jane's wishes.

Effort with purpose.

Years later, when I was talking about all this with a good friend, he'd confess to thinking how terrible the first scattering journeys must have been. I'd said that other than breaking apart and collapsing, my muddling forward, this moving deeper into grief, was the only thing to do.

Of the five places she wanted her ashes scattered, she never said anything about which one should come first. It probably didn't matter. But it mattered to me. There was the canyon country of southern Utah, which she'd come to know long before we met, confronting in that longwinded landscape an emotional struggle that had nearly killed her. There were the magnificent Sawtooth Mountains of Idaho, where we'd fallen in love and later married. Also a little cabin in the woods of northern Wyoming. And finally, two places in greater Yellowstone: the Lamar Valley, in the northeast corner of Yellowstone National Park, long a touchstone to the work Jane loved; and a certain high alpine lake in the northern Beartooth Mountains of Montana—symbol of the place that, after much wandering, we'd come to call home. I decided to first go to the Sawtooths, to begin the hard goodbye at what was our starting place. The place where we'd become a couple.

* * * *

I LEFT ON A FALL MORNING WHEN THE BEARTOOTHS WERE shining, capped by a fresh smear of snow. Driving through our town of Red Lodge seemed normal, which even four months after Jane's death was confusing: Merv the photographer walking down Broadway on his way to the bakery to sip coffee and swap jokes. Brad, looking serious in his orange patrol belt, waiting to guide the next batch of school kids over the crosswalk. Norm, wearing his one pair of brown Carhartts, stooping over in front of the coffee shop, combing the sidewalk for cigarette butts. Suzy out washing the front windows of her store. Mr. Bill strolling up Broadway with his hands in his pockets, trolling for conversation. Long before we had ever set foot here, a friend in Idaho had told me over a beer that this small town in Montana was a friendly place—not overly impressed with itself in the way towns in beautiful places can be. That's part of why we had stayed.

And yet we had come here from southwest Colorado in 1987 mostly for the surrounding lands: the far northeastern edge of a nine-million-acre tract of more or less undeveloped territory. The largest generally intact ecosystem in the temperate world. A place of snowfields and grizzly bears and whitebark pine forests, of elk and wolverines and mountain lions and moose.

Beside me on the passenger seat that September morning was the box holding Jane's ashes. Made by a friend up the canyon, a former Forest Service ranger named Rand Herzberg, it measured six by eight inches—a combination of aspen wood, blond and delicate, rimmed with strips of clear cherry. It was simple but elegant, graceful, so much so that it eased a little the uncomfortable feelings I had about what it held inside.

Speeding up at the edge of town, I cranked up Crosby, Stills, Nash & Young on the tape deck; with the palm of my hand resting on the box, I could feel the rhythm of Dallas Taylor's drum pulsing through the wood. Then the song "Helpless" came up, with Neil Young crooning about a town in north Ontario, and how "all my changes were there," and I ended up having to pull off the highway for a few minutes to get myself together. I stayed on the shoulder through "Our House," with its lines about two cats in the yard, about how life used to be so hard but now "everything is easy 'cause of you." Thankfully, "Almost Cut My Hair" came on after that, and with David Crosby letting his freak flag fly, I was finally able to drive away.

Like most couples, our relationship had a soundtrack. The year before we were married, by the end of our first summer together in the Sawtooths, we couldn't make the hour-long drive to Ketchum without Willie Nelson's *Red Headed Stranger* or Bonnie Koloc or Jean-Luc Ponty in the cassette deck. Jerry Jeff Walker and Emmylou Harris were well matched to the slow, full-hipped curves of the downriver road, and if not them, then Tim Weisberg or Stan Getz. Meanwhile the long, 128-mile trek west to Boise allowed everything from Ella Fitzgerald to *Hotel California.*

The fall after our first season together in the Sawtooths, Jane headed off to do her master's internship at a nature school in Michigan. Working by pay phone from Stanley, I managed to secretly arrange for a musician in Grand Rapids to meet us in a city park on a certain Saturday. Then I stuck out my thumb, making for the Midwest. East of Denver I got a ride from a truck driver named Big Daddy, and after a half hour or so of small talk he asked if I'd be interested in learning to drive a semi. Sure, I said. So he pulled off on the shoulder of Interstate 80 and switched places with me, then set about teaching me just enough about shifting gears so I could keep us rolling across the prairie while he nodded off in the shotgun seat.

The song I hired the musician to play for Jane on that Saturday in September was Judy Collins's "Since You've Asked." The singer was blond, in her late twenties. She took her place on a park bench on that sunny afternoon and smiled at the two of us, strummed her guitar, and began to sing. Afterward I thanked her and shook her hand, pulled from the pocket of my sport coat a white envelope with forty bucks in it. She tucked the money into her guitar case, said a quick goodbye, and walked away. Then I pulled out a folded handkerchief, spread it with a flourish on the green grass, got down on one knee, and asked Jane to marry me. I gave her seven roses that day, handing them to her one by one, each with a promise. The second rose, the second promise, was that I'd always protect her.

Now, some twenty-five years later, I was scattering her ashes.

After the town of Columbus came three hours of freeway, then blue highways again just east of Butte. All strangely quiet. Not a single car came on or off the interstate in Reed Point, or in Big Timber, or at the three or four off-ramps marked as ranch exits, each pegged with a blue sign with the words "no services." The movement, that lonely whine of tires on open roads, was a gift. For the first time the memories were just a little less suffocating. The grief ran down the highways with me—a mix of tenderness and sorrow that shifted with every passing town, with the far side of every mountain pass, at every place where pavement turned to dirt.

* * * *

FOR A TIME WHEN WE WERE YOUNG, IT SEEMED OUR WHOLE generation was moving. Leaving home. Leaving town. And while Jane was fond of wandering, for me it was an obsession. And if at the heart of that peculiar nomadic age I was too young to stick out my thumb, I did what I could.

Starting when I was thirteen, with my brother fifteen, every Monday of summer vacation our parents would let us hop on our bikes for daylong meanderings. And it didn't matter how far we went. Fueled by Corn Flakes and toast slathered with Smucker's strawberry jelly, the two of us—sometimes with another friend or two—gathered the five or ten bucks we'd each made mowing lawns the previous week and started to ride, my brother on a Schwinn Super Sport and me on a twenty-four-inch purple five-speed Sears Stingray. First we exhausted destinations with the coolest names—Shipshewana, Diamond Lake, Wawasee—followed by trips to more practical-sounding places like Michigan City, Syracuse, Goshen. Sixty, eighty, a hundred miles in a single day.

We left from Twenty-seventh Street in River Park, pushing off from our tiny house past the tiny houses of our neighbors—as often as not, heading west. In ten blocks came Potawatomie Park, with its greenhouse and little zoo of crowing peacocks and snorting donkeys—the place where our mother said when I was around three, I got so entranced with a geriatric lion that she and my grandmother couldn't get me to move. Finally they started walking away, thinking it would prod me to come along. I wished them well, so the story goes, then got back to enjoying the big cat.

A block later came the grand brick edifice from 1940 that was our high school, visually prominent thanks to a curious, medieval-looking tower that once housed a radio studio where Kate Smith stood and belted out "God Bless America." From there it was twenty minutes to downtown, cruising past the department stores—Robertson's and Gilbert's ("where one man tells another"), as well as the Masonic Temple on North Main where at twelve I earned $25 as a trumpet player playing the "Charge!" refrain for three guests being honored for some civic accomplishment, long since forgotten. Then past the old Palace Theater, in 1940 host to the World Premiere of *Knute Rockne: All American.*

And in later years, to a terminally groovy teen dance club called the Top Deck, with black walls and fluorescent cartoon paintings, hosting pop bands from Tommy James and the Shondells to Archie Bell and The Drells and The American Breed. It closed the year I started riding my Stingray past, after two sixteen-year-old boys were stabbed to death out front on the sidewalk.

Soon we were pedaling through the west side of town, and there the neighborhoods were poorer. Along with the usual scatter of Hot Wheels and doll buggies on the frost-heaved sidewalks, the lilac bushes and the Laundromats with revolving signs—things you'd see on the other side of the Grand Trunk Railroad tracks, as well—here there were cracks in the pavement, more broken glass and debris on the shoulders to steer our bikes around. Now and then there were little scrap yards tucked between the houses with the carcasses of a half-dozen cars scattered about, maybe a washing machine and a couple refrigerators, a beat-up bicycle on its side in front of a General Electric range, rolls of wire and piles of boards and strange gasoline-powered machines the size of suitcases. Tiny bars squatted on every other corner, their faded white Hamm's signs hanging in the smoky windows. There were fluorescent hair salons, and markets with cardboard boxes out front filled with tomatoes and potatoes and onions and apples. There were liquor stores and gun shops with iron grates in the windows. And out on Western Avenue, women in short skirts with lots of makeup, trying to be flirty, looking like they hadn't slept in a long while.

Finally, in the northwest corner of the city, past Mayflower Road, South Bend just fizzled out in that blessed way of smaller cities, replaced after ten minutes of no-hands riding by empty roads and fields of corn. Now came the smell of cut alfalfa and ditches full of chickweed. The mew of catbirds in the raspberry bushes. The gossip of blackbirds on the telephone wires. We'd crossed the wall of the city, as psychologist James Hillman once called the boundary between town and country. People in trucks waved as they passed, as did old retired couples out sitting on their porches. Riding at a steady ten miles an hour, which was no big feat for about any bike with air in the tires, by lunch we'd routinely find ourselves some forty, even fifty miles from home. Under our own power. Calling our own shots.

Early in the afternoon we'd pull into a Dairy Queen or Tastee-Freez, dismount the bikes with our chests puffed out, and swagger to the window to order a Mr. Misty, our skinny legs poking out of our shorts, hoping somebody would take notice and ask where we were from. But they almost never did. The one guy I recall striking up a conversation with us on the outskirts of Michigan City did raise his eyebrows when he heard we'd started forty-five miles to the east, but not in a look like wow, that's great—more like geesh, you guys must be stupid. We took a pull from the straws in our drinks, made an authoritative check of tire pressure with our thumb and forefinger, remounted, and pushed on, ready for the next amazing thing, knowing full well that we were having the most fun of anybody in the world.

The older I got, the farther I went. And not just for adventure.

I needed reassurance that the world didn't demand or deserve the brittle distrust my mother gave it, that I could fling myself to the winds and end up being blown to good places. By my senior year in high school, I was hopping into boxcars, rolling west out of South Bend on Friday nights toward Laporte and Chicago, or else north and east, through a string of small towns that would eventually lead me all the way to Detroit.

Riding rails was the ultimate "backyard" travel, offering glimpses of things never meant to be seen; over the years I saw couples rolling around naked on blankets spread across the lawn; a man in the garden kneeling between rows of lettuce, crying; an old woman passed out in the ditch, clutching an empty bottle; two teen boys standing next to a clothes line, kissing. In college I rode further still, drifting out of Bloomington, Indiana. Late one night in July, riding through a thick forest in southern Illinois in an L&N boxcar, the train reached a long, high trestle. About a hundred feet below was a narrow valley, about as long as a football field, filled with hundreds of thousands of lightning bugs. As the boxcar creaked out across that trestle, every single one of those flashing bugs paused for a couple seconds, pulling the valley into black. When they started blinking again, it was in perfect unison. Blink, dark. Blink, dark. Blink, dark. They were still doing it when I finally lost sight of them, when the train plunged back into the trees, making for Effingham.

When I wasn't in boxcars, I was hitchhiking—sometimes five or six hundred miles on a weekend for no other reason than

I didn't have any other plans. I traveled with next to nothing. On one trip I left Bloomington, Indiana, in 1976 for the bicentennial celebrations in Washington, D.C., with $1.36 in my pocket, hitching all the way in one ride, courtesy of a guy in his twenties in a candy-red Triumph TR6. In my junior year of college, a friend and I attempted to sail to the Bahamas in an English catamaran. We'd wrangled it for $250, rebuilding it through the spring on the back lawn of our apartment complex. We returned home from that outing early, turned back by storms on the ocean. One evening, my mother took me into the backyard, asked if I remembered how when I was little she used to point to a wink of light on the north horizon, telling me it was my star.

"Remember me saying how that star would watch over you, keep you safe?"

I nodded.

"Don't wear it out."

But by then I was out of her hands. Nothing for her to do but pray for me—that, and try to stifle the dark rumble of disquiet she still carried about the unreliability of the world. She'd been a dreamer once, smitten as a girl with the idea of becoming a professional singer. But at nine she lost her father, and then, just two years later, after tending her bedridden mother during a long bout of congestive heart disease, that parent was gone, too. Suddenly orphaned, she and her older brother, Junior, huddled together and made a solemn pact to stay with each other always, no matter what. Soon afterward, a big, dour German uncle came by the house where they were staying, stood in the living room with his arms crossed. After several minutes sizing up the siblings, he pointed to her brother.

"We can use Junior," he said. "Can't use her, though."

Of course she knew I was a dreamer, too. Years later, I had the surprising thought that maybe she took that belt to me because she'd come to know, at a young age, how awful life could be for those who expected too much from the world. As if those big expectations led to the cruelest pains of all.

Yet there was no knocking it out of me. On an ill-advised first date in my senior year of college, I remember talking to the young woman across the restaurant table about how someday I wanted to walk the length of the Rockies. She poked at her salad, bored. Then she asked me when I was going to grow up.

That only made me want to go more.

* * * *

STILL THREE HUNDRED MILES SHY OF THE SCATTERING grounds, I pulled in for the night south of Anaconda, Montana, along Doolittle Creek, a fifteen-minute drive on a dirt road branching off the highway toward the tiny town of Wisdom. Just me in deep woods at the foothills of the Pioneer Mountains, the floor of the forest rife with the silky leaves of sedge and Solomon's seal. Beyond the trees was a long roll of grassland dappled with Black Angus, and then the foothills, rising for several miles toward the highlands, tossed with thick clumps of Engelmann spruce and lodgepole pine. Exactly the sort of place Jane and I and Abby the traveling cat camped hundreds of times. I tried to read but couldn't focus. Tried to write. But mostly I stared into Doolittle Creek, gurgling through a clear, sand-bottomed pool stirred by fingerling trout.

My routine on the scattering journeys would end up much the same as when the two of us were together. First a cold beer from the tiny fridge in the back of the van. A little cheese, some chips and salsa. Beans, or maybe a stir-fry dinner, cooked on a Coleman stove given to us as a wedding present in 1980, the meals always served up on the brown porcelain cowboy plates Jane bought in that same year to mark our new life on the road.

After cleaning up, doing the dishes, came fires. As great as it was across our twenty-five years to be on the move, no less pleasing was no movement at all; as often as not, fire was the bridge from one state to the other—sitting up late at night at the edge of some black woods, or in the mouth of a chiseled canyon in the Southwest, or even nestled in front of a small blaze under spruce branches, in a hollow of snow. Fires had even been a part of the work we did—burning slabs of pine for happy tourists in the Sawtooths, and later in Yellowstone, spinning tales for them about bears and volcanoes and trappers and legendary snowfalls. Sometimes on New Year's Eve we plucked pieces of driftwood from the riverbank, decorated them into Yule logs, and tossed them into the flames. In the mid-1990s I learned how to fashion a bow-and-drill fire set from pieces of sagebrush. Even now I go out behind the house and twirl the spindle against the fire board with the bow until a tiny ember forms, lay it into a kind of bird nest made from juniper bark, blow it into a blaze. "Mother giving fire," as a Paiute elder once described it to me.

Late that night on Doolittle Creek, sipping on a short bourbon and poking at the fire, I recalled a conversation Jane and I had shortly after we were married around a small blaze at the base of a run of slickrock in southern Utah. It was cold and the sky was the color of ink, pricked with stars—sometime around midnight, in the hour when old memories come down to hover at the edges of the flames.

"I was sixteen," she said. "Struggling. One day my boyfriend just ended it. Right when I'd been trying so hard to be perfect." She looked up from the fire to catch my gaze, brushing the bangs off her forehead, tucking them under the edge of a blue bandana.

"I thought if I was perfect, the world would be perfect, too. That'd be my reward. Proof from God that I was doing a good job."

That night was the first time she talked of her mother being the daughter of an alcoholic—child of a man who abandoned his family when she was just a girl. And how, for a long time before he left, Virginia had this strategy of not making waves, of pleasing. Thinking she might keep that last straw off of the camel's back. Jane said she picked it up, too—this sometimes-desperate feeling of not being in control.

Meanwhile her father, though he'd later mellow, was a hard-boiled perfectionist. Fierce in his expectations. And very serious about that notion common to the rural Midwest, which says appearances are exceedingly important. His lawn was clipped.

His house and wife and kids and tractors were clean. His furrows were straight as good lumber.

She leaned forward and stirred the fire, gathering embers from around the edges of the ring. "I made mistakes. I was sure I'd failed the family. Failed my boyfriend. Failed the whole town."

She was in high school when the anorexia started, though back then no one called it that. For two years she sat at the dinner table picking at the pot roast and potatoes and corn and cottage cheese, then excused herself to tie on tennis shoes and slip out the back door to run six miles along the county roads that framed the farm. At night she went to the bathroom, locked the door, and gobbled down ex-lax. I later saw photos of her from that time, alarmingly thin, showing the dim, weary eyes of the underfed; always with a thin smile, though, maybe for the benefit of whoever was taking the pictures. When she finally started eating again, at seventeen, she fell off the other side of the fence, gaining more than eighty pounds in under a year.

"People didn't know what to say. I went to see the pastor. He patted me on the shoulder, said I looked good with a few pounds on."

Then one night, in some dark bottom where even now I can't imagine her, out of energy and ideas, she choked down a handful of sleeping pills.

She woke up in the hospital, her parents standing beside the bed, the two of them worried and fumbling, trying to be encouraging. Her father looking slightly embarrassed. But more than that, like he was about to cry.

"There was a lot of love. They couldn't get it, though. But then neither could I."

There was no more purging, but she kept running, still using the six-mile loops along the cornfields and woodlots near her family's farm to hold on to some feeling of sanity. And there was therapy, too—lots of hours spent trying to figure out what she wanted and, in particular, what she wanted for herself. She also started perusing what was for nature lovers a kind of underground reading list of poets and scientists and storytellers: Gary Snyder, Wendell Berry, Loren Eiseley, John Hay, Aldo Leopold, John Muir, Edward Abbey. Works that invited her to go outside and reconsider things she'd long been told weren't open to reconsideration. Over time, things got a little better.

Around that late-night fire in Utah, she also talked about going back to Kentucky as a counselor for the Girl Scouts. And how, from then on, the work seemed different—how there was this feeling of seeing smiles on the faces of girls who didn't have much to smile about. Poor girls. Abused girls.

"They didn't see going outside as a vacation, or as some kind of time out from school. It was more about making peace with the world." The fact that the woods didn't judge, didn't condemn, didn't expect anything, was never lost on them. All they wanted—and by then, all Jane really wanted, too—was to find a place that would let them in. And nature was always willing.

But there was something else, too. The natural world, even at a summer camp, was uncontrollable, unpredictable. And yet unlike in the daily lives of those girls, here the unpredictability was pure, utterly lacking in agendas. Nature had no intentions. It might sound odd, but more than a few of the struggling girls would, on first arriving, interpreted a cold, rainy day as some kind of punishment for their shortcomings. In a few days, though, they put such ideas away. They began to see that not every discomfort was their fault. They didn't want the bugs to be biting, but there they were. They would've preferred the headwinds to stop pushing against them while out paddling in the lake. But unlike when they had such thoughts at home, out in nature those kinds of wishes seemed a waste of time. Things just were as they were. And that difference made it easier to start thinking about their own lives differently—things they could do something about, versus things that for the time being they had to learn to accept. There was enormous relief in that lesson. Powerful not just for those campers, but for Jane herself, who used it as a motivation to start looking for her next big outdoor experience.

Nine months after Jane's hospitalization, an older cousin with some strong back-to-the-land urges of her own happened to mention a program she'd heard about called Outward Bound. Jane liked the sound of it, sent off for a brochure. Among the saturated Kodachrome photos from the various courses the school offered were shots of southern Utah. She said it looked distant and outlandish beyond imagining. Bereft of any trace of the world where people measured each other by the straightness of their corn rows; absent, for that matter, every single ingredient she'd ever been told went into the making of a worthwhile landscape.

Years later I read to her something Daniel Webster said in the middle of the nineteenth century about that region, part of his argument against expanding railroads into the West. What could anyone possibly want, he growled to Congress, of that vast and worthless area? "That region of savages and wild beasts, of deserts, of shifting sands and whirling winds, of dust, of cactus and prairie dogs?"

She flashed a smile, then shot right back:

"The answer's in the question."

* * * *

I REACHED IDAHO ON THE BACK SIDE OF A WESTERN FIRE storm, rolling into the remote Stanley Basin two days past a burn that had already swallowed some forty thousand acres. The day before my arrival, though, some relief—an early season snow, laying down the smoke and ash to reveal brilliant views of the Sawtooths. With every passing hour, the smell of charred wood gave way to the peppery scent of live lodgepole and to the sad, sweet fragrance of wheatgrass curing in the meadows along Valley Creek, the stalks brown and still in the September sun.

Nearly all the tourists had been sent packing or were warned away. Except for the morning and evening comings and goings of firefighters, the tiny village of Stanley hovered just above a ghost town. Closed signs hung in the windows of our old haunts: The Sawtooth Hotel, where we ate our first forkfuls of sourdough pancakes. The Rod and Gun Club, where on summer evenings in the late 1970s, Casanova Jack belted back whiskey, climbed onto an old wooden stage at the back of the bar, and, bedecked in a white jumpsuit, became Elvis, or at least Elvis on Quaaludes.

I'd barely heard of these mountains when, desperate to find some kind of outdoor job during summers in college, I spotted on the campus of Indiana University a poster by the Student Conservation Association—a fresh, feisty little nonprofit dedicated to matching young people to conservation jobs in parks and forests across the country. Having sent away for summer listings for 1977, I squeezed into a tiny coffee shop in Bloomington on Kirkwood Avenue one afternoon to study the possibilities. The job I ended up with, listed in a section covering the Sawtooth National Recreation Area, promised the duties of a naturalist: taking tourists on nature and history walks, entertaining them at night around the campfire. Still, as good as all that sounded, other places had similar offerings. So that evening, I unfolded all the appropriate western-state maps on the kitchen table in my apartment—maps I'd started collecting when I was ten—analyzing which job locations had the fewest number of paved roads nearby. The Sawtooths, with a single major north–south highway squeezed between two wilderness areas and one other similarly twisted piece of pavement heading west, this one closed in winter, by those standards seemed about as good as it gets.

The following summer I rolled west, hurtling out of the corn belt behind the wheel of a '64 Pontiac Tempest I'd named Stickeen, after John Muir's dog. Near the end of the first day of driving, on a sweltering afternoon near the outskirts of Kansas

City, in the middle of rush hour, the car let out a few short coughs and died in the middle of the west-bound lane of Interstate 80, leaving me to muscle it onto the shoulder. A couple minutes later, with the car on the roadside dead as a post, I looked in the rear-view mirror to see behind me a semitrailer losing traction around the curve, the trailer actually sliding akimbo down the shoulder some two hundred yards away and closing fast. I lay down on the blue vinyl bench seat of the Pontiac, cradled my head between my arms, and stared out the driver-side window, waiting for impact. But it never came. The trailer slipped by six inches from my outside rearview mirror.

I grabbed my wallet from the glove box, slipped out the door, and started hitchhiking, finally finding a mechanic's garage where a couple grinning red-haired teenaged boys towed me in and set about happily chewing their fingers on the carburetor and distributor. Well into the evening, and four test-drives later, they were no closer to a cure. The real mechanic, they finally confessed—a guy named George—wouldn't be in until the following day. And with that they hauled out a twelve-pack of Budweiser and invited me along for a fast twilight drive in a rusted brown Impala down a maze of county roads, the two of them taking turns seeing how many gophers they could run over during a single song on the radio. John got four during Thelma Houston's "Don't Leave Me This Way," while Mike, even with the benefit of something longer—I'm thinking it was the theme song from *Rocky*—managed only two. George came in the next day and fixed the car all right, but it took most of my cash. If it hadn't been for an odd east wind across Nebraska and Wyoming, I probably would've run out of gas money long before reaching the mountains of Idaho.

The next morning, in the middle of Wyoming, there came a kind of epiphany. It happened right before dawn, the light so weak I could barely make out the sagebrush and pronghorn and sagging lines of barbed wire unrolling along the highway, the pieces sharpening then blurring, a final smear of doubt before the world began to flare again in the June sun. Pulling off at a nameless ranch exit to piss out the latest cup of truck stop coffee, I found myself enlivened by new smells—this bright, bitter tang of alkali and sage. Gone was all trace of home: the lemony grease of furniture polish, the baked meatloaf with ketchup glaze and chicken casseroles floating in mushroom soup. Gone was the smell of ripe garbage and bags of grass clippings waiting in the alley for pickup on Tuesday mornings; the sour whiffs of rubber drifting through the neighborhood from the Uniroyal factory some thirty blocks away. In that empty reach of Wyoming, smells were no longer in service of unlocking the past, as Proust would have it. Instead, they made a strong case for kicking the past out the door and speeding the hell away.

I was neck deep in one of the most reliable of American seductions, the hunger for escape, which by the 1960s and '70s had reached religious proportions. One way people answered these siren songs was to move to places where they could drive up some gravel road, shoulder a Gerry Pack, and head up long twists of mountain trail. Like a lot of generations before them, they often carried a fervent, misguided hope that just by coming to a new place, they could turn into someone new. But even so, they were falling in love with the American landscape. And their love affairs led to an explosion of wilderness preservation, giving protection to more than thirty million acres of unfettered land in the '70s alone.

Unfortunately, the relationships weren't always strong enough to last. Maybe it's like falling for someone solely for his or her good looks, the love firing but then fizzling like a bottle rocket. Too often we forgot about those people in Gary, Indiana, at the edge of the steel mills, or those along the chemical alleys of Louisiana and New Jersey, too poor or otherwise disenfranchised to leave. Our blunder wasn't blowing off the environment. It was in failing to cultivate a dream big enough to include environmental justice. We never really grew the windy stories of our youth into something more substantial, more suitable to adulthood—something with a greater measure of relationship. And because of that botch, we lost the chance to gain millions of urban allies.

* * * *

WHEN I AT LAST ROLLED OFF INTERSTATE 80 IN THAT SUM-mer of 1977, heading toward the hot-lava plains of southern Idaho, I couldn't imagine the great upheavals of earth waiting for me three hours to the north. I crested Galena Summit in late afternoon, some thirty miles from the ranger station where

I'd be working, pulling the old Pontiac off to the side of the road and walking out to the lip of a knee-buckling ocean of mountain peaks. A land fresh out of creation. Pink and gray granites pushed through ancient seabeds in massive upwellings, fractured along vertical lines into what appeared like the deep, rugged teeth of a crosscut saw. And then the handiwork of great tongues of glacial ice, beginning some fifteen thousand years ago, carving a fantasy land of high-mountain-lake basins, hanging waterfalls, and steep arêtes.

Jane would come two summers later, heading out from Indiana to spend the summer with me before starting work on her master's degree. We'd met on campus at the last possible minute, in the final three weeks of undergraduate work, the two of us teaming up with another young woman for a class project. Jane had noticed me before that, though, she said later. But only because of the ridiculously loud ticking of my pocket watch.

"I thought maybe you were going to explode."

She told us she was longing to get back West—was thinking of checking out California. Maybe you should try Idaho, I offered. Her plan was to direct a YWCA camp in Indiana for the first half of the summer; then, later in the fall, she'd begin a post-graduate internship in Michigan. Come out to Stanley in August, I said, promising to help her get a job for the last month of the summer, to pay her rent.

In early June, a week after I landed back in Stanley, I got a call at the ranger station.

"Is that offer still good to help me find a job?" she asked, going on to explain that the summer camp she was supposed to direct was abruptly canceled.

"It's still good," I assured her. Then after work, I headed down to talk to a woman who'd been advertising for a hostess at the Mountain View Café. I called Jane back, told her the job was hers if she wanted it. And in what she later swore was the first spontaneous thing she'd done in her adult life, she took her savings and bought a ticket and the next day headed west.

* * * *

IT WAS HARD TO MISS THAT STANLEY WAS HAPPILY BEHIND the times. Much of what was most appealing about the boomers' early love blast for nature was still simmering in modest little towns all up and down the Rockies. The poorer the place, the more inclined it was to welcome coveys of young drifters with a little money in their pockets—many who, like us, ended up as seasonal workers in the adjacent national forests. For a few golden years, ending in the 1980s, there was a kind of sweet camaraderie between the newcomers and the old-timers, prompted in part by how much the boomers needed older residents to help them figure out how to live. Especially in winter, in what were still fairly primitive conditions: Where to get firewood. When to plant a garden. How the hell to keep a truck—or, God forbid, a Volkswagen—running at forty below.

An old friend of ours tells of being stuck in Crested Butte, Colorado, when the water pump on his old Dodge van gave out.

He says he knew he was home when a group of complete strangers hailed him off a neighborhood street and invited him to a backyard barbecue hosted by a family of Croatian miners, complete with accordions and tambourines.

"Here were these hippies and old-timers all mixed together," he said. "I'd never seen that before." It took about a week to replace the water pump on his van. He finally rolled out of town seven years later.

Stanley, too, was that kind of place.

There were few televisions in the Sawtooths. No private phones or computers or movie houses or bowling alleys or game rooms. By night, Jane and I were either out in the backcountry or in bars drinking Rainier and dancing to a stereo blaring out Hot Tuna and New Riders of the Purple Sage. On days off, we floated the river or, more often, hiked the mountains. We came to know each other at three miles an hour. Up Slate Creek, or across Railroad Ridge in one week, off to Baron and Alice and Twin lakes the next. We listened to each other's stories about home. And at every turn, we confessed a need to forge a life that would keep wild ground always underfoot.

* * * *

IT WAS EARLY AFTERNOON WHEN I PARKED THE VAN AT IRON Creek and brought out a small, chocolate-brown earthen vase, maybe six inches by four with a ceramic cap, hand-thrown years ago by a friend who's an amateur potter. Into that I spooned a measure of Jane's ashes from the wooden box, taped the lid shut, slipped it into the top of my loaded backpack, and began to walk. From the dirt parking area, the trail rose toward a granite basin hidden in the high peaks—the first place in the wilderness the two of us ever visited together. That time, there was ice still float-ing in the lake, and Jane dared me to jump in. Which of course I had to do. Which of course left her obliged to follow suit.

But now my trek was playing out to a soundtrack of red squirrels and Clark's nutcrackers, flitting and chattering and squawking, frantic to build storehouses of pine seed for the com-ing winter. A whitetail doe spooked from a patch of fireweed, breaking the limbs off a fallen tree as she disappeared into the forest. By the time I reached the lake, though, after nearly two hours of steady climbing, the world had gone strangely quiet, no buzz or chirp or scurry. I sat on the shore for a while, thinking about early mornings with Jane still asleep in the tent, catching brook trout for her from these very waters and frying them up with grits and eggs. At one point I'd told her this was one of the places I wanted my ashes scattered, too.

The lake was just like I remembered it. A jewel.

On two sides, steep walls of broken granite rose eight hun-dred feet from great piles of talus—places too raw and unsettled to support much in the way of life other than patches of lichen, the occasional clump of fireweed. But on the other shorelines were clusters of lodgepole pine, straight and handsome, the toes of their roots curling through thin soil just a few feet from the water's edge. Where the forest opened, patches of brown grass fluttered, along with the dried stalks of what a few weeks ago were gardens of wildflower blooms. And from those gardens came the voices of two streams: the inlet to the lake, arriving in big cartwheels out of the jumbles of rock, then the outlet on the other side, harder to hear, in less of a hurry, easing over a loose scatter of stones and then on through thick mats of sedge and rush and horsetail.

I'd never scattered a loved one's ashes before. And in the long minutes before actually doing it, there seemed a clatter of meaning and uncertainty greater than any heart could bear. In one minute my breath was running ragged, heaving up sobs every time I had the thought that this would be it, the final proof she was gone forever. Never again would her fingers touch my shoulder. No more embrace. No more rolls of laughter. No more smell of campfire smoke in her long brown hair.

But beyond the sadness, I was frightened, too, aware that while I was seeing and hearing and smelling the lake and the grass and the trees, I had no real comprehension of them. No joy, no story. Like a man waking up without memory or understanding, unable to differentiate a smile from a frown, an embrace from a slap, a laugh from a cry for help.

And yet every now and then I broke free, climbing above the sadness and the fear to become ennobled—by the five-hundred-mile drive, by this walk into the high mountains, supremely honored that it was I who'd been chosen to carry out this precious woman's last request. It was in one of those times, with that particular feeling on the rise, that I slipped into the jar a silver serving spoon from my late mother's one treasure—a table setting given her on the day of her wedding by the aunt who finally agreed to raise her when she was orphaned at thirteen—and stepped to the very edge of the lake. Then it began. The sight of a fine mist of ash floating in slow motion down the shore, across the fireweed, and finally brushing the cold cheek of the lake. Also, the faint sounds of a patter of tiny bone chips hitting the water and fluttering through the shallows, shards of oyster white, disappearing at last against an embroidery of granite stones. The sun was a gift, warm on my face. And yet there was an old, familiar sadness too, knowing the winds of October were on their way—soon to churn the waters of the lake, soon to fasten the water with a layer of ice that would last all the way to the following June.

A friend in southern Utah has for years managed great comfort from the thought that on his own death and cremation, the molecules of his body will be released, taken up by hundreds of other life forms. "That's immortality, brother!" he once told me. On the shore of that lake, I wanted to believe I could see it too. Maybe next spring, some infinitesimal iota of Jane's ashes would be taken by a freshwater shrimp, snapped up a week later to become the fin of a brook trout. Then maybe the trout would get plucked from the water, becoming the feather of an osprey; the osprey passing too in time, and with its demise that same jot of matter washing down Iron Creek to the Salmon River and on to the Pacific. And maybe in some autumn far away the same molecule would rise as rain, drifting eastward in the belly of a cumulous cloud until the Sawtooths pushed it up and cooled it into snow. There it would rest until the following summer, when the June sun would melt it, sending it tumbling back into the belly of the lake.

Hydrogen and oxygen, fueling the alchemy of forever.

Despite my best efforts, though, it would be a long time until any of that brought comfort, when I could see as beautiful the fact that hidden within the passage of Jane's remains were the forces of life itself. For the time being, that was little more than background. Like gravity, or the sunrise, or a thousand other things going on without me.

Just as I finished the scattering, a perfect feather the color of cottonwood bark drifted down, shed by a Clark's nutcracker circling overhead.

"Is that you, Jane?" Which brought an immediate response from the bird—the usual squawking, like an old lady who smokes too much, clearing her throat.

I lifted my head and called back. "I miss you. A lot."

WATER TO STONE, TWO

I stumble with my broken leg up to the rim of the cliff ledge that brackets the rapids, some forty feet above the river. Looking until my eyes ache, yelling her name into the roar of the rapids. Twice I step on what seems like solid ground only to fall through carpets of moss—once slipping over the lip of the cliff, grabbing the branches of a small conifer to haul myself up again. Of course the busted leg isn't much use. But the pain isn't registering. It takes me nearly an hour to make the two hundred yards to the point where we flipped and then back again. As usual we've made a safety plan, this time with the guy shuttling our van. If he doesn't get our telephone call by nine tonight, he'll alert the authorities. But it's ten thirty in the morning. And I'm not about to wait ten hours for help.

Then, a kind of switch gets thrown. My mind suddenly goes totally, fiercely rational. At one point I start thinking something's wrong with me because I can't connect any more with the panic that's been rumbling in my gut since the wreck. Back at the flush pond I tie up the canoe—so if Jane shows up, she'll know I'm okay—grab a bottle of water and a couple of energy bars, a white plastic bag to signal for help. I splint the broken leg with a straight piece of balsam wood and two Velcro straps, fashion a crude crutch out of a paddle, and begin the three-mile trek out. But the entire landscape is blocked by chest-high downed timber. So mostly I crawl.

I'm 150 yards along when all of a sudden two loons back at the flush pond begin making the strangest, most outrageous commotion—a cacophony of titter and echo so far beyond the usual loon delirium it stops me in my tracks. Shreds all my rational thinking. For reasons I can't begin to fathom, I spin around on the makeshift crutch and hobble back, feeling all over again the muddle of dread and hope and terror.

It's hard to express what happens at the pond. The two loons are there, sitting together on the upstream side of the flat water near the foot of the rapids. At my approach they go silent. Leaning on the paddle, I'm suddenly overwhelmed by two ideas, two images. Not thoughts—not like whispers overheard in another room. Something deeper, speaking not to the ears, but to the bones. A second or two later I shut it out, muster all my energy against it. The message is lovely beyond imagining, heartbreaking beyond belief. The message is "Beautiful. Goodbye."

IN THE SWEET MIDDLE
OF NOWHERE

With Jane's death, I decided to cancel almost everything, at least for a few months—speaking and teaching events, writing projects. During my entire career, choosing subject matter to write about was easy; the whole world, especially the wild world, was like a candy shop, with far more threads to follow than there was time for following. But all that was driven by a sense of wonder. And for now the wonder was out of reach. Not that nature was absent. On most any given day, certainly back here in the Sawtooth Mountains of Idaho, all I had to do was open my eyes to see it everywhere. But it was hard to feel the mystery of those wild places. I could see some of the brilliant ways things functioned here, sense the overwhelming complexity of it all. But none of that carried enough heat to spark the poet fire.

At the same time, the world at large seemed irascible, edgy. In August, more than 1,800 people died in Hurricane Katrina— the disaster putting a spotlight on an even bigger disaster, having to do with being poor and black in America. Car bombs were going off all over Iraq. Arnold Schwarzenegger was grating his veto pen across a same-sex marriage act. The Environmental Protection Agency was caught blacklisting scientists said to pose threats to pro-business ideology.

Closer to home, the first wolf hunts were getting under way. Not satisfied dispatching the animals with bullets, some politicians were pushing to allow the use of poison gas for killing wolf pups in their dens. Others, not so well versed in the Constitution, called for the nullification of the federal Endangered Species Act. And despite the fact that in all of North America only two people had been killed by wolves in over 150 years, Oregon politicians were rallying the troops for an outright war, calling it "a battle for the safety of our families and communities." So it was good to be back in Stanley for a while. In part to escape, I suppose. But also, hopefully, to wake up.

After the first scattering, I'd planned to spend the night in the backcountry. Instead, I walked out. After a summer in a cast, I felt like moving, pushing through the discomfort of my broken foot twisting and turning and finally swelling against the trail, opting for pain over the damnable numbness. Then again, maybe it was just too hard to be out in the wilds, when the wilds seemed so much less than they'd been the year before.

So I drove out Valley Creek, instead, to the meadows where we were married. Some sixty people had come for the wedding, two-thirds of them friends and family from faraway places, standing among the flowers and staring open-mouthed at the snow-covered peaks jutting into the June sky. Jane's five-year-old niece, Vanessa, was the flower girl, stealing the show prancing around the meadow in her pink dress, filling out her bouquet by plucking camas and sego lilies and buttercups and shooting stars. Jane's father, meanwhile, seemed remarkably happy to find cow patties lying in the grass; we guessed they reminded him of his beloved Angus cattle, back home in Indiana.

I'd intended to ask Gilman for his daughter's hand in marriage all proper like, but I never got the chance. On getting out of the car in their driveway for the first time, Jane swanned over to her parents, gave them big hugs, and by way of introductions told them, "Mom and Dad, this is Gary. He's asked me to marry him, and I said yes."

I stammered and blushed like a Hoosier tomato.

"If it's okay with you, that is."

She was "Janey" to her father, able to coax out his boyish mischief in a way no one else ever could. When they came together after months apart his whole body seemed to exhale, as if with her there, it was okay to stand down a little, indulge his weariness. Gilman treated me with enormous kindness, which I always thought generous, given how hard it must have been to watch me climb behind the wheel of the Chevy van and motor off to the Wild West with his precious daughter. But then, he'd been there with her when she was in such terrible pain during her high school years. Now she seemed happy. And I think for that reason alone, he could let her go.

On the night of our wedding, with pieces of rice clinging to our hair, surrounded by smiling family and friends, I slid open the side door of the van, picked Jane up in my arms, and, with her giggling loudly, carefully placed her across the threshold. Years later I wondered if such a move might have been alarming as hell to her father and mother. But if it was, they never showed it.

My own father, meanwhile, was gathering his courage to deliver a toast at the reception dinner. He'd been a major player in our adventure, helping us back in northern Indiana through the bitter cold of January and February to convert Moby the van into what in all seriousness was the eighty-square-foot home of our dreams. He was a soft-spoken man, generous, incredibly talented but at times oddly unsure of himself. Definitely not a maker of toasts or speeches. The night of the wedding, though, he pushed his chair back from the head table, rose to his feet, slid his gray glasses against the bridge of his nose, and with a nervous smile raised a glass of mead to the bride and groom.

"Some marriages are made in heaven," he said. "This one was made in Idaho." And then he sat down.

Later my mother gave him grief, thinking the comment simple. Jane and I thought it was the coolest thing we'd ever heard.

It was in that summer when we made our first real journey in the big blue van: with curtains she'd made on her mother's 1935 Singer sewing machine, a Hudson Bay blanket from her childhood bed, a scatter of family photos tacked onto a cork board. At the end of the second day of driving, when we were surely and truly West, we stopped late afternoon near the mouth of the Yampa River Canyon, outside Colorado's Dinosaur National Monument. From there we climbed up and away from a lonely dirt road into a toss of slickrock, took off our clothes, and lay down beside each other on the warm rocks. It felt like coming to rest in the middle of a Gary Snyder poem.

Sixteen months later, in October, my mother called—sounding choked and out of breath. My father had been doing sheet metal work on the roof of an eight-story courthouse in Plymouth, Indiana. The night before was cold, below freezing, so when morning came, it was decided someone from the crew should test the metal roof for frost, make sure it was safe to work on. He volunteered.

Suddenly he was dead, broken to pieces from an eighty-foot fall. For years afterward Jane and I would lie on the bed of the van and stare at panel and trim pieces and stowage lockers—intricate puzzles of layout and cutting and assembly he'd solved, one and then another, almost without thinking. I still wonder now and then what it would be like to meet up with him again. We'd finally make up for that stubborn habit of men in the Midwest, of never talking much. I'd apologize for not fully appreciating his extraordinary patience. Tell him he was right when he stood in the bedroom door one night when I was eleven and told me that change of habit comes slowly, an inch at a time. Ask him why, in the face of my mother swinging that studded belt against my bare skin, he couldn't see his way through to protect me. Tell him how I wish he'd lived long enough to talk to me about the things that made him afraid.

* * * *

LEAVING VALLEY CREEK IN A WASH OF ALPENGLOW, THE SKY reddened by smoke, I parked the van along the Salmon River and settled in, then pulled out a small cardboard box from under the bed. Inside were the road and trail journals Jane and I had created over twenty-five years. They began in the summer of 1980, two and a half months after we were married in that meadow, so filled with camas lilies that from a distance it looked like standing water. Jane was busy working up ideas for her first natural history book for kids, which would be published the following year. I was typing out stories for small magazines, jumping on any idea that promised a few bucks and a trip down a dirt path or lonely highway. Somewhere along the way we hatched a plan to further stoke the romance with a 300-mile bicycle ride—from the Canadian border around the fine green edges of Washington's Olympic Peninsula. One afternoon in August, though, sitting on the ground in a patch of yarrow with a road atlas spread out in front of her—in a tone so casual she could've been reciting a grocery list—she said that while we were at it, maybe we should just go ahead and ride the entire West Coast.

Three weeks later we climbed onto our skinny leather bike seats in the town of Blaine, Washington, the bikes sluggish with cameras and camping gear, making for Rosarito, Mexico, six weeks and 1,700 miles to the south.

She wrote every evening in the campgrounds. Again in the morning over breakfast, noting everything from chainsaw carvings at the Wild and Woody West in Oregon to massive platters of pancakes and eggs and biscuits at the Samoa Cookhouse in northern California. She wrote of fearing for our lives in the snarl of the San Jose freeways, of thousands of monarch butterflies fluttering all around us at Pismo Beach, having flown there for winter from the cold places of Canada and the high West. She told how the buzz and clutter of Tijuana melted into a quiet Baja seacoast highway, thick with barrel cactus and ice plants and chaparral.

And there were a lot more notebooks in the years that followed. Snapshots from hundreds of meanderings—recording weather and plants and bears and bugs and tourist traps and story ideas and stray conversations. And while most of the entries are matter-of-fact, between the lines is a headstrong, busty affirmation of the one sure thing each of us brought into the marriage: that to the extent there was such a thing as deliverance—from too little money or too much worry, too little patience or too much snow and mud—it would come, and without strings, from the heart of some unbridled land waiting down the road. Within a few years we'd be off to write stories at Glacier and Chaco Canyon and Acadia, in the Grand Canyon, the Smoky Mountains, even the Arctic. Always returning to the home woods. Breathing in, breathing out.

In the early days, those stories were written in longhand on legal pads. Getting them ready to mail off to editors meant first entering them into a computer, then printing them—tasks that required spending a few days in private campgrounds with electrical hookups. We'd pull into some KOA, or Happy Joe's, or Bear Hollow, or Prairie Dog Village, then run one extension cord from outlets under the picnic shelters to our forty-pound Kaypro computer and another one to a massive thimble printer.

It was in those private campgrounds that we learned to work against distractions—televisions, generators, shuffleboard, bridge parties. In July of 1987, we spent a week writing at the KOA in Missoula, setting up next to a family living in the campground for the entire summer, the husband driving away from their tiny trailer early each morning for a construction job, leaving behind a wife, three kids, and a boisterous parrot. The problem was the parrot. Starting around eight thirty in the morning, it liked nothing better than to squawk out scoldings to the kids:

"Stop that, Mike!"

"Lucas, don't you dare!"

"I'm not telling you kids again!"

So it went, day after day, off and on through the late afternoon.

* * * *

WE GATHERED OUR NEWS IN THOSE DAYS FROM NEWSPAPERS
and AM radio stations, and sometimes, whenever reception
allowed, from National Public Radio. On rare occasions a line
about current events would make it into the journals: when
Sandra Day O'Connor became the first woman appointed to the
Supreme Court; when the catastrophe in Bhopal, India, happened, courtesy of a gas leak at a Union Carbide plant, killing
five thousand people; when El Niño was wreaking havoc, spur-
ring a fresh round of suspicions among scientists about the effects
of greenhouse gasses. We made a couple comments about Ronald
Reagan, too, mostly having to do with environmental matters,
questioning if he'd been AWOL for junior high science class,
having claimed on two separate occasions that living trees were
causing more pollution than humans—giving off not oxygen,
which of course is what trees really do, but carbon dioxide.

After the big bike ride down the West Coast, we signed
on to caretake a small ranch in the bitter heart of a Sawtooth
Mountain. That February, the thermometer stuck crazy close to
forty below. Leaving at the end of the job on a trek to Texas to do
a magazine story about cactus thieves in Big Bend National Park,
we passed through Phoenix. It was warm. The sun was shining.
You couldn't find a snow bank if your life depended on it. Six
weeks later, we drove into the Valley of the Sun in a van filled
with six cubic feet of worldly goods, planning to stay for a year or
two. We shut off the engine just after noon. It was 114 degrees.

Jane was quick to land a job teaching at a day care center;
two weeks into it she planned a special treat for the kids that

involved me dressing up in a Smokey the Bear outfit borrowed from the local Forest Service office. I climbed into the van—a van without air conditioning—the thermometer at 119 degrees, wearing a fuzzy brown wool suit, pushing through heavy traffic and the occasional wave of nausea for five miles before reaching the school. Panting in the parking lot, I paused to gather my strength, slipped on the Smokey Bear head, and walked into class. At which point every kid in the room screamed like someone just tossed scalding water on them, then ran off to find someone to hug, or lacking that, to hide in the coat room or the art closet or the bathroom. Several made for the door. The director asked me to leave.

We lasted in Phoenix for seven weeks. And even that was accomplished only by driving every weekend three hours north to the ponderosa forests around Flagstaff, crawling out of the van door on Saturday mornings and almost falling to our knees with how delicious the air smelled, scents like vanilla and butterscotch leaking from the bark of the trees mingled with the lemon and pepper of pine needles on the forest floor. By June we were asking for caretaking jobs in the more remote northern portions of the state. Anything to get back to the woods. Finally, at a bar outside Flagstaff, a middle-aged man listened to our tale of woe and told us to go to the Mormon Lake Lodge, ask for Fat Jack.

Pausing from his work at the bar restocking bottles of George Dickel and Jack Daniels, Fat Jack listened to our story. Satisfied we were determined, or at least rightly desperate, he told us to get ahold of a guy who owned a remote cowboy line camp twenty miles south of the Mormon Lake Lodge. Then he scribbled a name and phone number on an order ticket, pushed it across the bar.

"He might be looking for someone to keep an eye on the place through the winter."

The following weekend, in a meeting at a Denny's over a stupid amount of weak coffee, forty-year-old Joe Lockett sized us up as only Western ranchers can, then got friendly, then got to the point.

"There's no electricity," he said, mouth turned down under a thick mustache. "And once freeze-up happens in December, there'll be no running water. You'd have to use the spring tank, 'bout three hundred yards from the old cookhouse."

The cookhouse was the only building inhabitable, he added, though not by much. The nearest neighbor was seven miles away. In exchange for watching the place, we could live rent free. We told him it sounded perfect.

So another notebook was added to the road notes and the trail journals, this one to chronicle the cold, bright days at Lockett Ranch. We would stay there from the fall of 1980 to the spring of 1981. As I read the pages today, they seem overplayed, loaded with all the gush and giddy-up that comes from being in your twenties out living under open skies: Describing long ski treks at midnight through the aspen woods, the white trunks of the trees shimmering in the moonlight. Or cooking cornbread and beans and potato soup and chili and pots of spaghetti on top of a sheet-iron woodstove. Being under the blankets on an old wrought-iron bed from 1936 and listening to Bruce Williams from Talknet Radio on KOMA—eight hundred miles to the east, in Oklahoma City—with a battery-powered radio. There are even notes about the outhouse, covered floor to ceiling with horse pictures from a 1950 issue of *The Quarter Horse Journal*—35¢ a copy, three bucks a year.

Just before the snows came, while out on a morning walk near the cabin, a beautiful little calico Manx cat wandered up out of nowhere, apparently abandoned by her owners. By the end of the day she'd decided to move in, trading nights in the woods, which were growing colder by the week, for a little company, a down quilt, and the occasional bite of cheese. For her part she sent the cabin's rats packing, flushing them from the attic in a single day, when I'd been trying and failing to scare them out for weeks. One morning, long after winter came in, for some reason she started shaking, trembling. Not knowing what to do, we decided to seek help from a vet. So we carefully wrapped her in a laundry bag and climbed on the snow machine, only to have her at the end of the first mile let go a pint of piss all over Jane's lap, which in little time turned to yellow ice. The vet said the cat was fine.

While Jane continued to work on still more kids' books, I composed queries for magazine stories—sitting under a chest-high bank of east-facing windows, plucking at an old Remington manual typewriter on a plank table. Once a week we'd load manuscripts, shopping lists, and laundry onto a wooden sled cobbled together from stray boards found around the cookhouse, then ride off by snowmobile seven miles through the frozen forest to the van, which we then had to dig out with shovels. In Flagstaff I'd found an elderly lady willing to rent us a room with an electric outlet for forty dollars a month, and there I re-typed every query letter and article on a spiffy blue Royal electric typewriter my parents had given me the previous Christmas. At the end of the day we dropped the queries and manuscripts off at the post office and went to do the laundry and drink beer at the Flagstaff Suds and Duds, grab a Mexican meal at Poncho's. Finally, long after dark, we drove back to the parking lot and fired up the snowmobile, then rumbled through the woods, making for home.

Before the storm cleared, I wrote after one such trip, *eighteen inches of sticky white snow was pillowed on every post, pine, rail, roof, stump, and aspen. The world tonight is soundless. No whining of wheels on a nearby highway. No shouts, barks, or banging doors—no squeaks or grunts from machines. Across the room is a faint twitch of burning embers in the woodstove. Beside me, Jane's slow and rhythmic breathing, an occasional rustle of bedcovers as the cat gets still more comfortable. And that's all. Outside are seven miles of timber and waist-deep snow.*

The gusto ran unchecked in us all that fall and through the winter at Lockett Ranch, not crumbling until the late spring of 1981 with the arrival of mud season: too much snow on the roads to drive, not enough for travel by snow machine. *Hellish transportation problems have walled us in,* we noted on April 3. *Consumed by a severe case of cabin fever. Little things have become big: The damn leaky drain. Ashes floating around from our cast iron smudge pot called a stove. The water line breaks, forcing us to melt snow. We bitch, and on some days don't find a damn bit of comfort from being in this together. Need to escape, but can't afford to.*

Three weeks later is a one-line entry from Jane, every word in capital letters: *TODAY WE DROVE IN ALL THE WAY.*

* * * *

IN MAY OF 1981, WE LEFT LOCKETT RANCH FOR GOOD. Rolling out of the aspen woods of northern Arizona for the last time, we surfaced to find a wave of dark fantasies taking hold of the mountain west, spreading up and down the Rockies like so much blister rust, courtesy of a radically conservative group called the Sagebrush Rebellion. In the process, they were unwittingly helping to lay the groundwork for a new brand of gunslinger greed. Sagebrush Rebels were rough-hewn, angry, sometimes-violent white men, many having come to the West fairly recently, hoping to grasp some imagined glory from the good old days. Rather than seeing themselves as outcasts, they were the chosen ones. And as such, they wasted no time wrapping themselves in God and flag.

Their first priority was to declare war on evil. On one hand, evil in the form of the federal government (in particular, land management agencies like the Forest Service and the Environmental Protection Agency), and on the other, environmentalists. While the movement was never large, its effect was greatly amplified by a piling on of wealthy industrialists and their attending politicians, well aware that fueling a populist-looking war against evil government workers and environmentalists was great for keeping the West friendly to corporate profits. By the mid-1980s, extractive industry had become the main funder of the Wise Use movement, each year pouring millions into the cause.

Among other things, the Sagebrush Rebels demanded that federal lands in the West be given back to the states for development. Never mind that the states not only never owned those lands, but as a condition of statehood agreed to make no claim on them. Soon afterward came a much-publicized manifesto calling for mining and oil development in all national parks and wilderness areas, for logging old-growth forests and replanting them with species better suited to commercial harvest. And our personal favorite: eliminating protection under the Endangered Species Act for any plant or animal "lacking vigor to spread in range."

Meanwhile, their funding partners in extractive industry were sending millions of dollars to the Rebels through groups with names like Environmentalists for Jobs, founded by the Chicago Mining Corporation. In 1989, seven employees from Chicago Mining would force their way into a private home in Pony, Montana, harassing a group of locals meeting to discuss a proposed gold mine. Future meetings were held with a sheriff posted at the door.

Their message was as soulless as a Mad Max movie: Get rid of environmentalists. Weaken mine-reclamation standards and timber-cutting rules. Scrap the Endangered Species Act. Then America will be okay.

Twenty years later, during a project for *National Geographic*, I ended up getting a smaller, more personal version of such rusty bravado. The work involved walking 140 miles from my front door to the so-called most remote location left in the lower 48, there to spend three months in what I thought would be the modern equivalent of contemplating my navel. What I found instead was a handful of thug-like outfitters, illegally drawing elk out of Yellowstone National Park for their hunting clients to shoot by laying salt blocks just outside the border. They were also wasting the carcasses of the animals they killed, taking only the antler racks. A few were even raiding archaeological sites in Yellowstone and then selling off the goods. In short, using the wilderness like the Sopranos used north Jersey. Among the hooligans was a Bible-thumping, gun-slinging outfitter—a dangerous, feral sort who even law enforcement didn't want to touch. Going about the business of, as he put it, hunting for God. Still another outfitter discouraged private hunters from mucking about on "his turf" by secretly slipping pieces of elk carcasses under their tents when they weren't around, hoping grizzlies would come by at night and shred their camps. Mostly not native to the West, they were nonetheless proud to don the uniform, from handlebar mustaches to leather vests. And guns, of course—most hard-pressed to take a dump without a .45 strapped to their waste. Needless to say, they missed no chance to remind me that wolves were the spawn of Satan.

What was notable about the Sagebrush Rebels was their divisiveness. They struck with blunt anger, issuing death threats to federal employees, burning down Forest Service buildings, and later, in southern Utah, torching effigies of President Clinton, who had the audacity to create a new national monument there. If you weren't on the team, you were an enemy. At one point I too started getting threats, one round of telephone trash lasting several days, the guy on the other end telling me over and over again to "Lock and load. We're coming for you."

The Rebels showed up in Jane's and my road journals mostly as short notes about the bumper stickers they sported: *Earth First! (We'll log and mine the other planets later.)* And *Environmentalism— Just Another Doomsday Cult.* And *Going Green is the New Red* (complete with the Communist hammer and sickle). And in later years, *Reduce Carbon Emissions: Shoot an Environmentalist or Two.*

To be fair, the boomers who actually loved and cared about these landscapes could themselves at times be hugely irritating. We fell easily into great bouts of preciousness, complete with an embarrassing tendency to want to shut the door to development as soon as we moved in. We struggled, and not always with grace, to figure out where communities fit into the grand scheme of the wilds, too often stuck on visions of nature where people are strangely absent. And in the end we became part of a growing gentrification in the West, one that sent some of the best characters of the mountain towns, practitioners of the fine art of barely getting by, down the road to lower, cheaper, less spectacular country. It was under our watch that many of the last best places in the West became what were essentially gated communities. Class with one-way glass—safety first, unmarred by the sad places of the earth or the sad people who live there.

And yet for a lot of years, the devotion boomers had for this wild country left them more than willing to go to the mat to protect pristine rivers, to stop dozens of ill-conceived oil-drilling schemes on the tundra, to keep grizzlies roaming the hills of greater Yellowstone. They showed up at mine-proposal meetings and oil-drilling hearings asking the sorts of thorny, well-informed questions that left city councilmen and county commissioners mumbling into their coffee cups. And on some nights that took guts, as big, surly men wearing yellow armbands arrived thirty, fifty, a hundred at a time, brought in from faraway places on company busses to give the thumbs-up to whatever extractive project was on the drawing board. But the boomers kept showing up. And in the process, they raised the quality of discussion about natural resources to the highest, most citizen-driven level the mountain West had ever seen.

But as the Sagebrush Rebels were growing stronger, the boomers were becoming thirty-somethings with spouses, kids, and full-time jobs. Day-to-day life was revving up, getting faster. Circles of attention were growing smaller. Bigger, less-personal concerns we were happy to leave to anonymous authorities: the protection of grizzlies and whales and black-footed ferrets to wildlife biologists, the care of the planet to climate scientists, the upkeep of democracy to the free market.

And yet the free market was hardly friendly toward grizzlies or ferrets or climate change. Extractive industry, which had more or less been licking its wounds since the mid-1960s, had mastered the fine art of spin. By the 1990s, televisions were beaming images of comely white women in pressed lab coats, proudly showing off Exxon's or BP's latest clean-drilling technology. In the Rocky Mountains and Pacific Northwest, the message was more blunt and more sophisticated. Word spread fast that the thing to worry about wasn't the loss of more than 60 percent of timber jobs due to mechanization, but rather radical environmentalists pushing to save the spotted owl. Likewise, it wasn't corporate centralization of meat packing that had led to dwindling profits in ranching—forcing major increases in processing costs for rural cattlemen—but those fruity bastards who kept trying to protect the black-footed ferret, or the sage grouse, or worst of all, the damned wolves.

* * * *

IN 1982, WHILE READYING FOR A BACKPACKING TRIP INTO THE San Juan Mountains, Jane and I got word that seventy-six-year-old Kenneth Rexroth had died. He would be buried in Santa Barbara Cemetery—his grave the only one to face not inland, but toward the sea. His own words were etched into the granite of his tombstone:

> *As the full moon rises*
> *The swan sings in sleep*
> *On the lake of the mind*

So on the evening before departing on that backpacking trek, we paused long enough to read out loud to each other a little of his poetry. A small tribute to our fellow Hoosier. One verse especially, I still read every now and then:

Our campfire is a single light
Amongst a hundred peaks and waterfalls.
The manifold voices of falling water
Talk all night.
Wrapped in your down bag
Starlight on your cheeks and eyelids
Your breath comes and goes
In a tiny cloud in the frosty night.
Ten thousand birds sing in the sunrise.
Ten thousand years revolve without change.
All this will never be again.

* * * *

THE FIRST SCATTERING COMPLETE, I LEFT STANLEY HEADING north along the Salmon River, passing the site of that crooked little rust-red cabin that served as our first home after we married. I could almost see Jane walking out of the screen door across the sloping porch with a pan of blond brownies in her hand for the elderly landlords; how the first time she made them she forgot to consider the big lean of the floor, and so the batter slumped, making one side thicker than the other.

"It's perfect!" she told me. "People who like chewy eat from this side. Those who like crunchy eat from the other."

Five miles on, I pulled into a small turnout and walked down a steep bank to the edge of the river, to Cove Hot Springs, where I stripped naked and settled back into the steaming water, silky with minerals. Sitting in that hot pot, in a small way it felt like the scattering of Jane's ashes had released the Sawtooths back to me. Of course there was a lot of stumbling and lurching and bleeding in the bushes still to come. But after Stanley, I could begin to see a few of those things that outlast even the longest life. Some indigenous cultures of the world hold sacred certain corners of the land—never going there casually, reserving visits only for rites of passage. From then on, the Sawtooths would be like that for me.

Downriver some 115 miles was the town of Salmon, for decades a redneck-meets-river-runner place, serving up a kindly if sharp-edged brand of hospitality. During our first summer together in Stanley, Jane and I ran shuttle for river-rafting parties, driving their rigs from Salmon to a takeout on the river at Corn Creek. Our second gig involved shuttling a pair of Olympic gymnastic coaches from Salt Lake City who each year ran the river, then spent a drunken night at the Owl Supper Club. Afterward, for reasons we never understood, they bedded down in sleeping bags for the night—as did we—on the fifty-yard line of the Salmon High School football field.

For old times' sake, I parked the van and walked over to the Owl, sidled up to the bar, and ordered a beer. The place was quiet, just one other customer—a sixty-year-old man named George, sporting a gray ponytail down his back, humming to the country music feed on the television while flipping through a copy of the *Salmon Recorder Herald*. George wanted to talk. Before my glass was empty, he'd invited me to come back on Sunday to watch football.

"I cook up a bunch of chili—enough for everyone. People come and go all day, eleven in the morning till nine at night. You should check it out."

Salmon was for a long time less gentrified than other mountain towns, having for years had the good fortune of ranking lower on the groovy scale. There'd been less of an onslaught by well-meaning folks who move to beautiful places and set about trying to make them a little "nicer"; maybe pushing to get rid of the trailer park at the edge of town, for example, never understanding that such housing is all some locals can afford. But then Salmon was also more than happy to irritate the refined by spitting and pulling out guns at the mere rumor of wolves. Or environmentalists. Or any other commie scum predator lurking at the edges of town.

When Bill the bartender heard what I'd been doing up in Stanley, he turned and poured himself a beer, pulled up a stool behind the bar, and sat down to face me. Five years ago yesterday, he told me, he had lost his own wife. Her name was Jamie.

"A vein ruptured near her heart. The medical team didn't do the right diagnostics. Just never picked it up. She was forty-eight."

He took a pull on his beer and turned his head, and the look of pain on his face seemed fresher than five years would allow. Sitting there, just me and Bill and George the chili cook, some dozen blocks from the football field where Jane and I and the gymnasts had fallen asleep after way too much tequila, I began to realize how long a man's wounds can bleed.

The scattering journey in the Sawtooths was powerful, a right action of sorts, an honoring that suggested my life still mattered. But it wasn't long before holes started showing up, letting in feelings that everything was still busted to pieces. One of those holes tore open during that encounter with Bill at the Owl Bar. Earlier in the day I'd been going along thinking I was getting back to some sort of mental fitness, reclaiming what I'd learned from storytellers, psychologists, seekers of one sort or another. I could see myself getting on with recovery, confident I was coming out of the ditch, steering back into life. But as I left the Owl Bar and was heading north on Highway 12, making for Lost Trail Pass, it seemed that was just wishful thinking. Mind play. And minds never could fathom the real consequences of a broken heart.

WATER TO STONE, THREE

I'm moving down the west bank of the Kopka again. Even with a bib wet suit on, I'm starting to chill; pulse and breath are getting faster, shallower, making me think about shock. The nearest highway is a long hike to the east, and reaching it will mean swimming the river. Yet in the canyon below the flush pond, the far bank is almost vertical, impossible to navigate on two legs, let alone one. So I keep pushing downstream toward the mouth of the river, finally reaching the place where it empties into Obonga Lake. Slightly up from the mouth is a small island. After weighing the options, I decide to jump into the river upstream and float on my back to the island; from there I should be able to haul out and recover a bit, before tackling the second half of the channel. Everything goes well. Then, less than ten yards from the island, I'm sucked into a circling current. It carries me right back to where I started.

The shivering and shallow breathing are getting worse.

Resting a couple minutes to steel my courage, I jump this time into the river downstream from the island, which means making the entire crossing without a break. The water is fast and deep, the current much too strong for me to hold my place by swimming. Sure enough, even before the halfway point, the current catches like a train and hauls me far out into the lake. I'm exhausted. Just as that outbound journey comes to an end, a pair of loons surfaces not ten feet away. They eye me for a few seconds, then let loose with a brilliant run of yodels. Given how cautious loons are around humans, even in my troubled state it's not lost on me how strange this is. What I do with it is set my jaw and take a couple fast breaths, blowing them out like a man angry, like a man trying to convince himself there's still something left. I roll onto my back under the gray sky, lay the paddle on my chest, and start backstroking, pulling hard for shore.

At long last I heave onto the bank, rest just long enough to drink water and choke down an energy bar. From there it's back to crawling and stumbling over downfall toward the Armstrong Highway. In thirty minutes I manage only a few hundred yards. Then a sound. Faint, but growing. The thin drone of a boat motor, somewhere near the east end of the lake. Filled with hope, I lurch to the shore, practically falling into the water in my rushed attempt to get out beyond the overhanging tree branches to a place I can be seen. Sure enough, in the distance is a speedboat, and it's coming my way. Several figures are visible. Fishing rods are sticking up along the gunwales.

When the boat gets a couple hundred yards from shore, I slip the white plastic bag I've brought over the canoe paddle and begin waving it frantically, all the while shouting at the top of my lungs. No sign they see me. Next I put the paddle under my arm, and with two fingers in my mouth let out the loudest, shrillest whistles I can muster, followed by still more shouting and paddle waving. The boat never slows, never varies its course. Just keeps skimming westward at full throttle. I damn near weep.

Just as I'm about to step out of the lake and start moving again, I hear the boat's motor slow, see the fishermen pull in toward shore on the far side of the Kopka River, maybe a half mile away. I wait until they cut the engine and then begin frantically whistling, shouting, and waving all over again.

After ten minutes of this they start heading toward me, slowly at first then picking up speed. The men are clutching bottles of beer, and when I finally get the chance to sputter out what's just happened, they offer to take me back to their camp along the highway. When I hand my paddle to the guy in the bow of the boat, I can see he's pretty loaded, though that hardly makes him less appealing. At least not until he grabs the shoulders of my life jacket to pull me over the bow and slams my nuts into the hull. I lay on the foredeck in fetal position, hands clasped between my thighs, writhing. The guys think it has something to do with my broken leg.

They're paramedics, on a holiday fishing trip. Back in camp they prop me in a lawn chair on the beach, give me a blanket and a beer and a Darvocet for the pain, cut away my wet suit, and ice the broken leg. For some reason their satellite phone isn't working, and after several failed attempts, one of them runs up to the highway to flag down a car. The first driver spots him and speeds by, eyes straight ahead. Ten minutes later comes another one. This time the lone woman driver stops, makes a call to the Ontario Provincial Police.

The pain is coming on strong now. Not just in my leg, but in my back, too, which I'll later discover is covered with massive bruises and abrasions from being slammed into rocks in the Kopka rapids. My chest is heaving like the chest of a little kid trying not to cry. I sit in that lawn chair for the next hour watching the sky until a small plane appears overhead, a search plane. Shortly after that comes an ambulance. The emergency team is extremely kind, and that calms me some. I even find myself starting to hope. But it's the hope of a desperate man.

FLOWERS IN THE DUST

O f all the wild places we imagined going when we were young, it was in the northern Rockies that we gained our first sense of the kind of creative bedlam long gone from the land of corn and clipped lawns and Putt-Putt golf. Snowstorms showed up in the Sawtooth Mountains even in July, and in late summer, wind squalls powerful enough to knock down hundreds of acres of trees in a single breath. In spring came the thunder of landslides ripping loose from the upper shoulders of the high country; later, normally modest creeks turned treacherous with melting snow. All of which helped forge personalities in the locals more expectant, matter-of-fact, outrageous. Even the kids seemed like ungentled horses, full of themselves. Local historian Dick D'Easum tells of a Christmas party in a Stanley store where a seven-year-old boy dashing about on his new bike ended up running at high speed into the branch of a massive decorated tree, nearly breaking his neck. D'Easum said the kid didn't even cry. Just picked himself up, turned around, and shouted to the crowd: "That's one hell of a place to put a Christmas tree!"

Our own oddball behavior—oddball by Indiana measures, anyway—had mostly to do with me writing stories gushing about the outdoors, and with Jane squatting in the sagebrush with kids, helping them figure out why snakes went into holes, imagining how a red-tailed hawk could look down from five hundred feet up in the sky and see the twitch of a mouse half the size of a Twinkie. In the early years after we came to Idaho, our more traditional neighbors, many of them ranchers and loggers, didn't always understand what we were doing. But they were always long on encouragement—wishing us well, saying they hoped it worked out.

Of all the people we met over the years who marched to a different drummer, none played a bigger role in our lives than our Forest Service boss in Stanley, Chuck Ebersole—a former career Navy officer, brilliant and effusive and ornery. If the Sawtooths and the White Cloud Peaks were our classroom, the place we got our footing as naturalists, Chuck was the blustery headmaster. Before mailing me the paperwork for my summer job in college, he scrawled excited notes all over the margins. On the last page of the employment package, under the signature of the forest manager, he penned in big letters with a red felt-tipped marker: "This is a Western flavored, pioneer-mining-cattle-ranching-homesteading-but-now-infiltrated-with-tourists area of the Old West. You're gonna love it."

Chuck had the face of a Pennsylvania Dutchman, strong nose and jaw, softened some by his habit of standing with one leg forward and slightly bent, sort of like a rock hero might do, absent the guitar riding sidesaddle on his hip. When in a good mood his habit was to whistle, always the same refrain, thirteen notes long, over and over. In my first month on the job, speeding down the highway with Chuck behind the wheel, he'd routinely look out the side window of our government-green Chevy Vega, slam on the brakes, and leap out of the car to run off into a nearby ditch or meadow or patch of forest. The sort of frantic behavior most people reserve for spotting bags of money or dead bodies.

But what he was reacting to were the smallest charms of nature. One time it was a patch of penstemon flowers, where with barely contained excitement he proceeded to point out the flower's one sterile hairy stamen, an adaptation that likely allowed bees visiting the plant to deposit more of the pollen they carried on their bodies onto the stigma of the flower. Another day it was a stream bank full of horsetail, prompting him to spin images of how the plant had been around some hundred million years, dominating the understory of the ancient Paleozoic forest. By the end of these lessons his hands and teeth were clenched in a kind of quivering euphoria, until finally he'd smack his palm hard against his green twill pants and gush.

"Jeeesus kee-rist, Gary, isn't that great?! I mean, that is goddamned really something!"

When he was in the Navy, at sea for months at a time, Chuck
would roll out of his bunk every morning at three thirty to study
for college correspondence courses, in the end finishing twice
the number of hours he needed for a degree. He waded ashore
with the Marines at Guadalcanal. While out in the Pacific, he
learned of a problem with the B-24 aircraft, a design flaw that
made it impossible for rear gunners to escape in the event of fire.
Using parts scavenged from a ruined machine gun, he fashioned
emergency window releases. The day after the invention was
installed, it saved the lives of five men in a brutal crash landing.
Next he busied himself creating a retractable camera-mounting
system for the B-24, complete with a makeshift dark room in
an adjacent bomb bay, turning the airship into a photographic
reconnaissance plane. He walked out of the Navy in 1964 with
eight bronze stars, a silver star, and a breast full of commenda-
tion medals.

When he landed in the Sawtooths after getting his PhD, his
unbridled eagerness led him not only to learn nearly every plant
and animal and bird and geologic feature you could shake a stick
at, but also a boatload of regional history. In the early 1970s, he
and his wife, Brady, hiked much of what would later become the
River of No Return Wilderness, carrying a tape recorder, inter-
viewing the last of the hermits still living off the major drainages
of the Middle Fork. Guys who would normally run off anyone
at the point of a gun would talk with Chuck for hours. He was

astonishingly curious, no less so than the average ten-year-old, and often envious of the hermits' calm, ingenious ways: their mule-powered washing machines, their water-driven grinding wheels, their newfangled bear traps.

From Chuck we heard historic tales from the old times: about Whiskey Bob the mailman, who each week made a three-day snowshoe trek from Ketchum over Galena Pass and across Scrapper Flat to Obsidian carrying fifty pounds of mail; done with that, he schussed fifteen more miles into Stanley for a few games of poker. The next morning it was back over the pass, often at thirty below, and on to Ketchum to pick up another load. Every week, all through the brutal months of winter. We learned too about a former owner of the Sawtooth Restaurant named Harry Giese who in 1882 had a greenhorn customer order the cod ball special and then not eat it. Incensed, Giese let loose with a stern lecture about how the food was perfectly good, and that by the way, ingredients were damned hard to get in these parts. When the customer still refused to eat the meal, Giese did what few restaurateurs would consider proper: he pulled out a gun and shot him in the leg. A jury later found Giese not guilty, reckoning that a man has a right to force customers to eat codfish balls if they ask for them.

With Jane and me, Chuck was walking, always walking— on Forest Service trails, in the tilted sage fields behind the ranger station, out at the ranch on Valley Creek he and Brady took care of. He talked about getting out of the Navy and hiking the 2,200-mile Appalachian Trail nonstop with his eldest son,

Johnny—incredibly, repeating the feat twice more, once with his youngest son, Mike. And on very rare occasions, in a voice so quiet we had to lean in to hear, he told of the day Johnny, a biologist for the National Park Service, was doing bighorn sheep counts over southern Utah when the plane crashed, killing him. It was the only tale he told where his eagerness, the usual piss and vinegar, drained away, leaving him looking like an old man with a broken heart. We sat next to him staring at the ground, not knowing what to say, hoping he'd find his way back.

The first assignment Chuck handed me—which he later handed to Jane—was to read and discuss at length Edward Abbey's *The Monkey Wrench Gang*. When the discussion part happened, over lunch at the ranger station, it was spiked with such fits of howling laughter that he finally had to get up and shut the office door to satisfy complaints from the receptionist at the front desk. Being a novel about a ragtag group of wilderness lovers in the Southwest driven to blow up that great engineering scourge of the twentieth century, the Glen Canyon Dam on the Colorado River, it was hardly official government reading. But Chuck had a lot of Ed Abbey in him, including his outrage over wild country being pillaged for profit. Sometimes it angered him to tears.

To a couple of fresh-faced Hoosiers like Jane and me, such behavior was incredible, though of course at age twenty we could hardly appreciate the cost. That someone could be absolutely brilliant at his job and at the same time buck an institution he thought gun-shy in the face of its own values—to us that was foreign stuff. It was one thing to meet an older guy who'd been able to keep his passions burning. It was another to watch him do so when it meant pissing off the people who signed his paychecks.

When they learned Chuck was about to retire, the Forest Service Supervisor's Office in Ketchum—long hostile over his general impudence—suddenly panicked, realizing they were about to lose a treasure trove of original knowledge, none of which had ever been recorded. Shortly before he left, they mailed him a blank cassette tape with instructions to lay down all the things he thought future naturalists should know. On the day the tape came, I followed him out to the parking lot of the ranger station, where he placed the recorder in the gravel next to his cowboy boot, turned it on, then started grinding his heel as hard and loud as he could right next to the microphone. He kept this up for thirty minutes. An entire side of a cassette. Beneath the anger flashing in his eyes was an almost beatific smile, something a little kid might wear when peeing in the swimming pool.

"Let's see what the sons-a-bitches do with that."

* * * *

I MISS CHUCK EBERSOLE. I MISS HIM FOR THE WAY HE NEVER stopped to think before taking his curiosity off leash, letting it whoop and holler and run around anywhere it wanted, no matter how silly it looked. I miss him tilting at environmental windmills, knowing full well that's what he was doing, but caring less about outcome than about the earthy gladness that came from shouting against atrocities. I miss him because he was fierce in his belief that "the other"—in this case, elk and deer and bears and osprey and mink and moose—deserved the chance to live out their potential.

He used to tell us how the natural world had taught him a lot about critical thinking, that it helped him build an "ecology of mind." Nature was unimaginably complicated, he said; just rubbing elbows with it encouraged fresh, diverse thinking. Nature taught people to be comfortable living with questions. And that, he told us, was in turn a good remedy for our tendency to oversimplify the world.

In his later years, mythologist Joseph Campbell—who like Rexroth lamented the trading away of story for illusions of security, of constancy—was asked if he thought America might ever again embrace some useful body of myth. Yes, he said. It would look much like an image of earth as the astronauts see it—a precious, fragile ball of life hurtling through space, undivided by political boundaries. Entire. Irreducible. Gloriously inconceivable.

Campbell would've loved Chuck Ebersole.

* * * *

I RETURNED HOME FROM IDAHO TO AN EMPTY HOUSE. EMPTY but for the two cats, that is, Abby and Ruby, who at least brought a little comfort simply by needing me to feed them and scratch behind their ears. The sun was far to the south now; around ten in the morning it spilled over the tops of the aspen forest and through the living room windows, bathing the interior of the house with honey-colored light. In some ways, the place had never looked better.

It took a couple of days to dial down from the road trip, to get used to the idea of not moving. I missed the sound of the tires on the pavement, the blur of wet ditches filled with cattails, the sight of the full moon on clear nights pouring through the windshield. I missed seeing kids playing in their front yards, and young men standing on the shoulders of the highways, thumbs out and smiling for rides. Back at home, I had to figure out how to be at rest again. After the sun went down, I read—James Hillman, and Joan Didion, too, who advised that we all had to "pick the places we don't walk away from." I read Tolstoy and Bukowski and Joyce Carol Oates and Jess Walter and Rollo May. I wasn't looking for answers. Just hoping to feel something stir.

A few weeks after I returned from Idaho, something big happened. Since Jane's death I'd been swimming against a noxious sense of betrayal. As if the wilds had done me wrong. Not that we both didn't fully understand the risk of being in the outback. We'd canoed together for twenty years, from Florida to the Arctic Circle. We were certified in swiftwater rescue. She was both an Outward Bound instructor and a wilderness EMT—jobs that in every season brought sobering reminders of the risk of wilderness. Still, having always been fed by the wilds, encouraged by them even on brutal days, it was incredibly hard to think of them as the stage for her death.

The change came utterly without effort, while sitting on a stump outside my house near the swing I'd made for her, under a canopy of autumn leaves. At one point my eyes came to rest on a dying old cottonwood tree on the other side of the creek. And in that moment, I began surrendering to the inevitability of the end of things. To the fact that not one of the trees in front of me, not the grasses underfoot or the chickadees flitting through the aspen, not the ravens circling overhead, could've arisen in the world without being tied to that same conclusion. Just as up in the north country, beside the Kopka River, balsam fir would keep growing old and tumbling into the currents, whitetail deer and coyote and woodpeckers would drop to the ground and have their bones picked clean and crumble into soil.

Grace seems to show itself more readily in the wake of grief, slipping into the room like a late-arriving lover and easing between the sheets. Who knows, maybe paying such close attention during that first scattering of Jane's ashes, mustering the focus it seemed to require, left me somehow ready for grace, better able to grasp some essential sliver of understanding. All I can say is, in what proved the first easy thing since the accident, I got off that stump and walked back to the house and through the kitchen door. And never again did I think of nature betraying me.

THANKSGIVING

Twenty years before our disaster on the Kopka, I'd been asked by a publisher in New York to gather a collection of nature myths from around the world—small, bite-sized stories about the making of earth's wonders. I talked to storytellers. Listened to old recordings by anthropologists. I went again and again into the stacks of major university folklore collections, combing through more than a thousand tales from every continent. Three months into the research it dawned on me that without fail, every story was holding up one or more of three qualities essential to living well in the world.

The first of those qualities was a relationship with beauty. The sort of relationship that grows out of quiet, intensely focused moments. Not shutting out the rest of the world; instead, being present enough to see the world through the shine of whatever beautiful thing is in front of you. The stories suggest that, while beauty may be fleeting, there is great reliability to it—a reliability so unerring, in fact, that it can pull the imagination to higher callings, to the outer edges of the eternal. Beauty is the moon Neruda wrote about, "living in the lining of your skin."

The second quality showing up in those stories was community—not just among humans, but with every aspect of creation. A sense of deep belonging—one that carries us out of the little room where loneliness lives into a wide world of ever-present embrace. Of sunlight in our bones and rivers in our blood.

The third had to do with the need to cultivate an appreciation for mystery, welcoming places or situations where the world seems utterly unfathomable. Not as some first step in figuring things out, but as the first step in giving up trying. It's a call to accept the fact that a great many curiosities about this life will never be answered, and further, that real peace is reserved for those happy to live day after day in the questions.

In that first winter after Jane died, I started rereading those tales I'd found: *Butterflies Teach Children to Walk*, given to me by an old Ojibwa woman; an ancient tale from Java called *The Forest and the Tiger*; and from West Africa, *The Birds Find Their Homes*. In recalling those three essential qualities needed to live well in the world, by making them what I thought about when I woke up and again when I went to sleep at night, I started to understand just what it was I'd lost touch with in the underworld of grief.

"Our stories hold life's lessons," said the Ojibwa elder who'd given me the butterfly story. "Bad things always get worse when you forget the lessons."

* * * *

SOME TWENTY YEARS AGO, JANE AND I WERE FINISHING UP THE last piece of trail from a five-hundred-mile walk around greater Yellowstone, part of a book called *Walking Down the Wild*. In the last hours of the day, pushing toward home down the Line Creek Plateau, we started talking about the most striking experiences we'd had in nature, not so much as a couple, but as individuals. The times that shaped us. First our minds drifted back to childhood. She recalled tents made out of sheets erected at the edge of her family's corn fields; I described how one summer when I was about ten, my brother and I had saved up our allowance to buy two pairs of green rubber boots, which we used in a patch of woods in northern Indiana, meandering up and down a tiny creek so small it didn't even have a name.

In the end, though, I told Jane the most striking experience I'd had in nature was in my late twenties, several years after we'd met, in the days when my mother was bedridden, dying of cancer. Having for a month been too weak to even hold her head up, she told me one morning she wanted to go outside. So I carefully gathered her up in my arms and carried her through the front door and out into the yard. Around we went for what must have been twenty minutes—first so she could smell the flowers on her lilac bushes, then so she could look through the woods above the bird feeder for the flash of a certain cardinal's wings. And finally, so she could run through her fingers the supple young leaves of the maples and dogwoods.

I'd never forgotten the solace my mother gained from that small journey around the yard, the last time I saw her alive. Having over the months watched disease whittle her soft, round body into something sharp and breakable, having seen the light in her eyes fade behind a wall of morphine, I found it hard to buy the claims I'd heard from Crow and Sioux people in the northern Rockies and plains who told me a person is never more powerful than when she's about to die. But on that day, she *was* powerful. By some special grace, she managed to harness the mystery floating through that quarter-acre yard and use it to light the dark place closing in around her. That afternoon, the pain she'd worn for so long began draining from her face, replaced by a look of serenity I'd never seen in her, even when she was young and healthy. The next morning she told my sister-in-law to stop all the painkillers, despite having been on massive doses of Percocet and morphine for several months. A few days later, in the still hours of the night, she drifted away.

The flash of that cardinal, the soft green leaves of the maples and dogwoods—they were small hints of the wild tapestry that once circled the earth, remnants of the patterns and paradigms that first breathed meaning into human existence. Hints that helped my mother transcend the tumult of daily life, offering her some slim measure of miracle, a hint of wholeness in her severed world. I too had been hunting for such inklings every time I'd gone to the wilderness. And most amazing of all was that I never once failed to find them.

I couldn't have spent the past thirty years watching saplings sprout from the ruin of fallen trees, seeing entire forests burn and then new ones rise from the ashes, watching the skies above Montana empty of birds in November and fill again in April, seeing its mountains pried apart by ice into boulders, the boulders into rocks, and the rocks into gravel and sand, without also surrendering to the fact that nothing we set eyes on, nothing we put our arms around, ever stays exactly the same. About this, the nature myths I'd collected from around the world were very clear. Of course there is a sadness in accepting that. But now there were days when it was a sweet, even comforting sadness. The kind of sadness that lies along the far edges of every love.

* * * *

DURING OUR YEARS IN MONTANA, WE'D MADE DOZENS OF SKI trips into small Forest Service guard stations and field cabins. And the one we visited most was a couple hours south of Red Lodge, in the southern Absarokas of Wyoming—two miles by trail up a remote river valley, cradled by Engelmann spruce and Douglas fir. We spent seven Thanksgivings there, each time arriving with backpacks topped with bags of turkey cooked the night before, mashed potatoes and canned oysters and cranberry sauce and red wine and cheese and salami and olives and French bread. And always too, ingredients for the one cocktail Jane was especially fond of on winter trips: the snowshoe, her version being a mix of Jack Daniels and a high-octane peppermint schnapps called Rumple Minze, poured into a Sierra Cup, chilled with icicles plucked from the roof.

Known as the Wood River cabin, this too was on the list of the places she wanted her ashes scattered.

I'd left in early winter of that first year, on a sun-drenched Thanksgiving morning, six months to the day following her death. Over the phone one of the locals told me there was no snow, not to bother bringing skis. But I arrived to find a good ten inches on the ground; with no skis or snowshoes, that would mean two miles of post-holing. Soon after leaving the parking lot and crossing the river on a steel footbridge, though, I crossed a lone set of prints from a big wolf. He was going south, the same direction as me, and the travel was made easy by placing my feet in the deep dents made by his paws. Except for a couple of short side trips, his route was unwavering. While at first I had to focus to match his gait, by the time I reached the big timber, maybe a half mile in, I could do it without even looking, stepping past the same downed trees and ice-covered rock faces he'd passed an hour or so earlier. When his tracks finally left the trail and drifted east across the frozen river, I was only forty yards from the cabin.

The place looked the same: A one-room cabin, twelve feet

by twenty, the walls made of small, unstained pine logs bleached by the sun. Along one outside wall was a pile of spruce and aspen wood taken from the surrounding forest, split and stacked, ready for the woodstove. Out in the yard was the same old freestanding sign board, meant to hold a forest map, but as usual, holding no map at all, which made weirdly profound the words carved into the bottom post of the empty frame: *You Are Here.*

Inside the single twelve-foot-square room were three wooden chairs and a small sink with no running water. Shelves too, with extras of everything from matches to lamp wicks, tampons to toilet paper. And on a flat board braced to the wall in the back of the room, several feet of books: Gretel Ehrlich's *The Solace of Open Spaces* and Bradford Angier's *How to Stay Alive in the Woods*; *The Virginian* by Owen Wister, a couple field guides, a fistful of *Daily Bread* booklets for those hungry for morsels from the Lord. And on the very end, Jack London's *White Fang.* The previous Thanksgiving, with the Coleman lantern burning, it would be the last book I ever read aloud to her.

What I was most interested in was the cabin journal, which Jane carried in on our first visit, making a gift of it to those who followed. Dozens of visitors used it, mostly families, many who like us ended up adopting the little cottage, caring for it by bringing in everything from rugs to stuffed chairs, lanterns to sauce pans. Though none of us ever met, across the years we came to know a little something about each other through the pages of the journal: Who catches fish and who snores. Who's good at spotting moose. Who trekked to the outhouse in the middle of a frigid winter night, looked up, and saw God staring back from the stars. I left a few new lines, letting everyone know that Jane had died.

Setting about the usual chores—filtering water, carrying firewood—as the last of the daylight leaked out of the sky, out behind the cabin I caught a glimpse of shadowy movement. Not fifteen feet away was a beautiful bobcat, her coat the color of dried grass. She walked slowly out from behind a juniper, coming toward me. Then she stopped and just stood there, staring into my eyes.

It was uncanny behavior, and once again I heard myself saying out loud, "Jane?" She considered me for what seemed close to five minutes—calm, blinking, swishing her tail. Then she turned and walked up the slope, disappearing into a loose stand of timber.

I didn't bother spinning theories about why one of the shyest creatures on the continent decided to give me such a long and careful look. I didn't sit in the snow and reconsider reincarnation. There was only the beauty of it. After the cat wandered off, I headed inside, poured myself a Scotch, raised the glass, and wished it well.

The next day dawned clear and cold. I heated up a little water on the Coleman stove, threw a teabag into a travel mug, put on a coat and hat and gloves, and walked down to the Wood River, and there began tracking the wolf I'd followed the day before. Still more ice had formed in the night, fanning out in teardrop shapes from the downstream edges of half-submerged granite boulders. The wolf had continued upstream, walking in a straight line, staying close to the water, finally veering off after a couple miles to begin a sharp climb into the gnarled foothills of Standard Peak. I could've followed his tracks all day, leaned hard into the effort, and I would never have come close to catching him.

Returning to the cabin, I gathered the vase from where I'd placed it the night before, in front of an east-facing window, pulled the silver spoon out of my backpack, went outside, and made my way around to the back of the cabin. Though it was probably ten o'clock in the morning, the air was still cold, sharp against my nose, smelling like winter. Maybe it was because I knew this would be the last scattering for a while, probably for months, that I stood for a long time out there in the snow, taking in every detail, trying to drive it into memory. But what registered wasn't so much details of the surroundings as a simple feeling of ease, contentment. As if, other than just being there under that cold November sun, standing calf-deep in the snow, there was nothing I needed to do.

After a time I moved up the hill, took out the spoon, and cast some of Jane's ashes on that east-facing slope. They fell without a sound, drifting like a thousand tiny feathers into the hollows of that bobcat's footprints.

WATER TO STONE, FOUR

I know that if Jane has any strength left at all, she'll do exactly
the right thing to stay alive. Having worked for years as an
EMT on search-and-rescue teams, not to mention teaching dozens of Outward Bound courses, she knows well matters of survival. She only has to be conscious. From the beach I can hear the
search plane droning in the distance, going up and down and up
and down the river canyon.

Late in the evening comes the thudding of another engine:
a helicopter, dispatched 150 miles to the south from a hospital in
Thunder Bay. It's come to carry me away. The paramedics carefully load me onto a gurney, lift it across the loose sand, and place

me into the cargo bay, strap me in. Incredibly, the pilot offers to fly the river canyon a few times so we can all look for Jane. Because I'm lying on my back, good views are hard to come by, but by raising on one elbow and twisting hard, I can peer out the side window, glimpsing the dark, broken conifer forest along the edges of the river. After three passes the pilot apologizes, says that with the light fading we have to make for the hospital. Jane will be spending the night out. It's getting cold. It's starting to rain.

We reach the hospital around 11:00 PM. There are X-rays, after which the doctor comes in to explain the nature of my broken bones; then a nurse shows up, fashions a temporary cast to stabilize things until I can undergo surgery back in Montana. Having heard the story of the accident, everyone is gentle, sympathetic, and I'm gulping the kindness. Around midnight a detective with the Ontario Provincial Police named Brad McCallum appears next to my bed. He's soft-spoken, courteous, even while explaining that for the time being, the accident has to be treated as a potential crime. He asks if there's anything I need from the van before his men seal it to protect evidence. We spend the next hour together, me giving him not only details of the wreck, but dozens of facts about Jane's habits and personality. The search team will use the information to create a psychological profile of her, in hopes of anticipating her movements, her behavior.

We finish around one thirty in the morning, and the detective offers to take me to a hotel. I've got no money or credit cards with me, but he thinks maybe the place we stayed before heading

out to the Kopka will still have my info on file. I've got no clothes
to wear, most of them having been cut off by the doctors; before
long, a nurse shows up with a baggy pair of sweat pants, a dark
green pair of underwear, white socks, and black tennis shoes. A
pair of crutches. When I'm finally dressed, I catch sight of myself
in a mirror on the wall of the hospital room. There's an old man
staring back.

At the hotel, McCallum takes a business card out of his wallet, writes his home number on the back, and hands it to me,
tells me to try to get some rest, to call if there's anything I need.
But rest isn't an option. I lie on the bed, crutches propped up in
the corner of the room, feeling a panic rolling through me like
nothing I've ever known. Little bits of hope rise now and then,
only to be devoured by images of her cold and bent and broken.
Or worse still, and this despite fierce efforts against it, a picture
of her at the bottom of that goddamned river—then the whole
world shrinking, groaning, the color leaking out of it like blood
from a bad wound, everything going to gray. My plan is to not
call anyone for twenty-four hours, not wanting to set off a chain
of unnecessary worry. Thinking mindless television might calm
me down, or at least distract me, I find the remote, and the TV
comes on to Country Music Television. A video is just beginning
to play. It shows a handsome young man, a performer I don't
recognize, singing a mournful song in front of a lakeside cottage.
A story unfolds about a wife, or maybe a girlfriend, who one day
was apparently out at the end of the pier when something went
wrong. She drowns in the lake.

By the next afternoon Jane's still missing, and I can't bear the load any longer. First I call her brother Tom in Indiana and tell him what's happened, having to repeat several things because my fast breathing is making me hard to understand. Then I call Martha, in Montana. Both say they'll catch the first plane to Thunder Bay. When people at the café Jane helped start with Martha hear the news, they take up a collection to pay for Martha's airplane ticket.

I'm getting regular updates from Detective McCallum, as well as from the search coordinator, a thoughtful, serious man named Greg Brown. We dig around a little on the motel Internet, learn that the Ontario Provincial Police Search Team has one of the best track records of any search team on the continent. Besides aircraft, there are three ground teams, including one with dogs—struggling up and down the riverbanks looking for her. Someone finds her paddle. Another searcher finds one of her gloves. They know Jane was a search-and-rescue worker. To my great comfort, they keep asking me for more information, for any ideas I might have about how she'd behave if badly injured. Greg says his men and women are motivated. He tells us as far as he and his team are concerned, they're looking for one of their own.

THE GREAT WIDE OPEN

Twenty-two years after Jane first came into that enchanted maze of canyons in southern Utah, beginning there her long waltz with Outward Bound, I had my own chance to see firsthand what country like this could do for the restless and broken. In my case, the lessons came by way of a bunch of highly intelligent, beaten-down, drug-addicted teens. In 1995, deep in the stacks of the University of Colorado library, I'd stumbled across early research showing that compassionate wilderness therapy (as opposed to punitive boot camps) was twice as effective for treating teen drug addiction as traditional twenty-eight-day lockdown. It was one thing to think of wild places as being powerful for those who sought them out. It was another to think they might also help kids who, at least on first arriving, would've rather been any place else on earth.

Hugely curious, I began writing a book on wilderness therapy in the spring of 1998. Among other things, it involved going through staff training at the Aspen Achievement Academy, located just west of Capitol Reef, then spending three months in the backcountry with so-called "at risk" teens, toggling back and forth between a group of fourteen- to seventeen-year-old girls and a group of similarly aged boys.

The kids had therapy sessions twice a week, which on the surface might not seem much different from how things happened for them back home. But out there, the therapist hiked in two or three or four miles to sit with kids under juniper trees. More remarkable still, she stayed with each one as long as it took, sometimes for hours. She was with us on the trail, climbing hills and tromping across washes. She ate her food out of a tin cup. Got smoke in her eyes. Huddled against the rain.

The field staff, meanwhile, included former instructors from Outward Bound. But there were also history majors, former addicts and alcoholics, musicians, even a chemist. Their modest wages aside, several told me they were here because they needed to work for a time at a job where they could give something back. Many had seen more than their share of struggle, often with addictions, and in the end decided the best way to anchor what they'd learned was to pass it on. Passing it on in the wilderness, they told me, brought a powerful sense of ceremony to the giving.

Not that they were wise or benevolent in everything, of course—
no more so than a lot of other twenty- and thirty-somethings
would be. But that desire to give back—that shining urge that
seems to wait at the end of so many heartbreaking journeys—this
they had in spades.

My first week in the field, I landed with a group of smudged,
sweat-stained fourteen- to seventeen-year-old girls. Kids wrestling with crank and speed and crystal meth, late-night trips to
the police stations, to the streets, to the suicide wards. With girl-
friends at school, in the toilets, throwing up lunch.

Like Nancy, who, among other things, was struggling with
bulimia. One afternoon, we were walking down a dusty trail
together, no one else within earshot.

"How could I deal with things if I didn't throw up?" she
asked me, her voice almost pleading. "What else is there in my
life I can control?"

She was at a level of the program known as coyote; one day I
asked her why she thought they'd named a part of the wilderness
experience for that particular animal.

"Coyotes are survivors," she said, and we walked on for a
long time, much of it in silence.

Later, before bed, beside the fire she started rapping on
the bottom of one of the tin cans we used to cook in. And then
someone else started in with thumbs against the bottom of her
blue porcelain cup. Then three more cups and a pair of wooden
spoons. Until there was this heady thrum drifting out across the
desert—in some minutes disjointed, in others, perfect. Right in

the middle of it, a coyote came up to the edge of the bench that ran along our camp to the south, gave three bright barks, turned, and walked away. All of us just sat there, looking at one another, amazed. Never slowing the rhythm, though, never stopping that drumming.

"That coyote," Nancy said the next morning over breakfast, as if only then was it proper to talk of it. "It was awesome." She slipped that memory into her pocket and she walked with it, all across the empty desert. Drinking from it like a spring, smiling over it when the weight of her pack, when the long, black nights, started pressing on her shoulders.

Now it was I who was broken, and in the years following Jane's death, Nancy and the rest of that little wilderness tribe seemed as close as I had to heroes. One spring I decided to get in touch with them again, some ten years after they'd made their final walks out of canyon country. One was working as an accountant, another a history professor. There were two nurses, a chef. Also an oil-rig foreman, an advertising executive, a furniture builder, a financial planner. They said things that Jane used to say. Seven of the nine told me their time in the wilds was still the most important experience of their lives. They asked me to remember how, out in the wild, everyone had needed each other. And thanks to that alone, for the first time in their lives, they had started thinking what they did might really matter.

Susan, a pediatric nurse, reminded me about how she came out of the canyons knowing it was okay to be different. I asked her if she remembered a certain biology lesson when we were in the backcountry together—ten of us in a circle under a cluster of willows at the edge of the Red Desert, the lesson offered up by a quiet, brilliant, sinewy sixty-one-year-old teacher named LaVoy Tolbert. Of course she remembered, she told me.

"Does everyone recall those big mushrooms we ran across earlier today?" LaVoy asked.

"Puffballs," Jenna said.

"That's right. Puffballs. And remember how we talked about them being a kind of life form that reproduces by spores—millions of spores, every one exactly alike?" At which point he slowly drew out their thoughts about the limits of such a life strategy.

"They're all vulnerable to the same diseases," said Jenna.

"If it's too dry," added Susan, "none of them survive."

LaVoy smiled, nodded. "So if I'm understanding you right, the only chance a puffball spore has is to land in exactly the right environment. Basically, the same conditions as the parent plant."

Then more discussion, with the girls acknowledging that most life doesn't clone itself like that at all, but reproduces sexually. A strategy offering nearly limitless potential for variety. And that with variety comes the chance to flourish in changing circumstances.

"It sounds like what you're really saying," LaVoy offered, going slowly, looking each girl in the eye, "is that nature loves diversity."

In the days that followed I watched girls who just the week before were bleeding from the jagged edges of all that had broken in their lives—the addiction and the fear, the violence and the abuse—staring out past the ponderosa onto the red rock of Capitol Reef, letting out breath, gathering up the pieces. Not unlike Jane, I suppose, out there on those cold November days in 1975, trying to shore up her riddled sense of self, struggling against the thought that not fitting in was a fatal flaw.

* * * *

DURING THEIR TIME IN THE BACKCOUNTRY, STUDENTS WERE expected to work toward high school credits for English and science. Though most were exceptionally bright, they tended to see themselves as almost dim-witted when it came to learning—something reinforced by their lousy grades. But that changed out there in the slickrock canyons. I watched as LaVoy turned their bodies into stand-ins for the planets and the moon and the sun, teaching them out there in the sand and the sage-brush how to spin and circle one another to mimic the patterns of the solar system. I saw them not only figure out what was happening when they twirled a sage spindle against a flat piece of wood and ended up with fire, but then go on to link the chemistry of combustion to the oxygen and hydrogen cycles in their own cells.

People from Henry David Thoreau to John Dewey, William Hornaday to John Burroughs, complained often about how American education—especially science—was too often divorced from actual experience. "One green bud of spring," wrote Thoreau, "one willow catkin, one faint trill from a migrating sparrow would set the world on its legs again." Science was tastier, the thinking went, and so more likely to be savored, when served up on a creek bank, scooping tadpoles and watching them under a magnifying glass, than it was sitting in a school room making borax snowflakes.

In the early twentieth century, Harvard and Yale actually contemplated starting "colleges of the wilderness," in large part because untrammeled landscapes were thought to be valuable stages for developing critical-thinking skills. Likewise the school garden movement, exploding around 1910, wasn't just about teaching kids where their food came from. It was also about taking advantage of the fact that children plunked down even in a vegetable garden were inclined to immediately start noticing things. And that, in turn, gave rise to questions: Why is that fruit red and the other one blue? How come some flowers close at night? Why do the bees disappear before a rain? How do plants know to come up in the spring?

A hundred years before Jane took her first teaching job at a nature-based elementary school in Michigan, the incredibly popular Agassiz Association, founded by celebrated biologist Louis Agassiz, was advising teachers to not overwhelm young kids by asking them to learn scientific names of insects and parts of plants and the like. Let them instead go outside and follow their innate sense of wonder. Sophisticated learning could come later. The group had another piece of advice, too—one that would've seemed awfully relevant to those kids in wilderness therapy: "Whether you are four or eighty-four, be an original investigator.

See things for yourself. Look into the thing, not into what has been written about the thing—what you find, not what someone tells you to find."

Jane liked to say that most kids got more from running a single maple leaf through their fingers than from scouring a hundred photos of trees in a textbook or on a computer screen. As outdoor education director for the Center for American Archaeology in Cortez, Colorado, she'd squatted in the sand amidst the junipers with fifth graders, helping them figure out where the best places might've been for ancient Anasazi to plant their squash gardens. Working as an instructor for Outward Bound, she'd knelt down next to fifty-year-old teachers and insurance agents and lawyers, picking apart piles of scat to see what the bears had been eating. And in Yellowstone, with the Park Service, she'd headed out with elementary school kids following wolf tracks, watched them tap their knuckles against petrified trees, helped them measure scalding temperatures in the hot pots and thermal pools and then figure out how something might actually manage to live there. Time and again, kids who thought they were slow, even stupid, came away thinking otherwise.

* * * *

IN MAY OF 2006, JUST BEFORE THE ONE-YEAR ANNIVERSARY OF the accident, against the welcome simmer of life back on the land, I readied to make another trip to scatter ashes. This time it would be to southern Utah, to an especially outrageous tangle of sandstone along the eastern edge of Capitol Reef National Park. It was the landscape at the heart of Jane's Outward Bound experience thirty years before, a special wilderness. The place, she once claimed, that had probably saved her life.

SLICKROCK WILDERNESS

I got a late start for canyon country, rolling south in the old blue van as far as Green River before pulling off in the wee hours for a little sleep at the back of an abandoned gas station, beside a sad toss of weeds and cracked concrete and rusted barrels. The rest of the night played out to the whine of big trucks on Interstate 70, some running for Denver, others heading west to Interstate 15 and on to California. Every twenty or thirty minutes one slowed and exited the freeway, rumbled past me there on the outskirts of town—pausing just long enough for a tank of fuel, maybe a microwaved burrito at the Gas-N-Go on West Main. Just passing through.

By sunup I was on Highway 95, making a sweet, lonely run along the eastern edge of the San Rafael Swell. Beyond the road were dapples of locoweed and purple vetch, dropseed and cheat-grass and fescue, here and there the occasional huddle of juniper or cottonwood. We'd always loved the feel of this Utah, scoured and sunlit and ornery and wild. The hoodoos of the Swell and the sweet-smelling ponderosa on Fishtail Plateau. The Virgin River Narrows of Zion. Those perfect groves of aspen forest near Sundance. The cold, snowy woods of Bear Lake.

Beyond its considerable enchantment, though, like a lot of places in the West, Utah has struggled mightily with the flotsam of progress. Salt Lake claims the fourth-highest toxic chemical releases in the United States; number twenty-four on the list is just thirty miles down the road, in the tiny town of Tooele. In the past fifteen years, the state lost over a million acres of farmland to development. And as I made my way toward canyon country, fundamentalist conservatives, joining their brethren in the north, were shouting at the top of their lungs about how any minute, wolves were going to start pouring over the borders and eating children.

I pulled in at the Mesa Market near Caineville, parking beside a small white storefront at the edge of a field brimming with vegetables. Inside, the place was spartan, decorated with a few wall hangings and painted gourds. The owner, Randy—a short, swollen man with thinning blond hair—offered me a salad from organic produce he'd just plucked from the greenhouse, topped with a boiled egg and a chunk of feta and a nasturtium flower, pushed up against a slice of warm homemade bread. It may be the best thing I've ever tasted. We talked a bit, Randy telling me that in another life he used to sell whirlpool baths and later hot tubs (a career impossible to imagine him in), lamenting how the job taught him that people have little sense of how to be happy other than by spending money.

"People never cared at all about how much the thing cost," he said, looking incredulous even now. "Only how much per month."

One day the boss caught him discouraging a prospective customer, something he apparently did fairly often, and showed him the door.

By local standards, even now Randy wasn't particularly well behaved. Over several years he'd fought at various public meetings, totally outnumbered, to force the Bureau of Land Management to develop a legally required land-use plan for Factory Butte, just outside Caineville—a plan meant, among other things, to protect fragile areas from dirt bikes and four-wheelers. Here there was no one to fire him for being a rabble-rouser. Instead, off-road vehicle fans promised to slash his greenhouses and burn his business.

When I finally told Randy why I'd come, he nodded, looking like he half expected me to say something like this.

"The most important thing," he said, "is to be present in the face of fear." Then he went on to talk about a good friend, a Hopi man who'd been advising him on planning a ritual he'd soon use to mark the death of his own partner, dying of cancer.

"My Hopi friend says helper spirits out on the land are bigger than what can be contained in human form. Actually, they're gigantic. But mostly peaceful."

The elder told him how such spirits showed themselves around smaller landforms, mostly located near prominent peaks and buttes. Randy let out a long breath, turned from the counter to put a loaf of bread in the oven.

"I don't know. Maybe it's something you can use."

West of Caineville the land melts into the bare bones of existence: rusted waves of sandstone peeling away with every passing storm; deep blue sky, hot and thirsty and bright. And wind, especially in the shoulder seasons, shouting down the canyons in March and April and then coming back around again in the fall, driving ice and sleet through the cold days of November. Just off the highway, pocket meadows no bigger than backyard swimming pools nestled against sweeping arcs of sandstone, tossed with the red of firecracker penstemon, the burnt orange of globe mallow. A lone juniper clinging to the east wall of Slaughter Canyon. Here at last, then, was the wind-shorn mix of rock and sky that so changed Jane, starting her on a path that turned her from a Midwest farmer's daughter into a full-blown woman of the wilds. The Utah of old. Timeless.

* * * *

WHEN JANE ARRIVED IN SOUTHERN UTAH FOR THAT OUTWARD Bound course, it was a spectacularly naive time for American wilderness programs. Hundreds of earthy young men and women—self-described "dirt bags"—were busy creating outings intended not merely to build skills, but in these last sweeps of open space to light some fresher, stronger sense of self. And their clients were hardly confined to late-blooming hippies; Outward Bound also attracted thousands of corporate executives, as it does today. Some came with coworkers, using the challenge of wilderness to bond with colleagues. Others came alone, needing one good blast of clarity before quitting the corporate world altogether, trading it away, usually against the advice of friends and family, to become a teacher, a nurse, maybe start a health-food store or a pet shop or a coffee bar. Jane talked often about that particular group:

"It's hard for anyone to follow their inner voice if they can't hear it," she said. "The wilderness just turns up the volume of what's most true for you."

Back in the 1970s, details of what constituted right and proper outdoor adventure were in flux, hard for the boomers to nail down. For starters, how could programs that promoted living off the land—a metaphor for self-reliance, which often involved eating plants and small animals—be reconciled with their own fast-emerging ethic of leaving no human trace of ever having been there?

Then somebody got the bright idea to spare the wilderness with chickens.

The chickens were used mostly at the end of courses like Outward Bound, when each student was asked to catch one darting about in the sagebrush, wring its neck, then pluck and cook it. This activity, it was hoped, would satisfy the goal of building self-reliance. Of course there was the not-so-minor problem of getting live chickens to the middle of nowhere in the first place. Larry Wells, at Brigham Young University, hit upon the idea of delivering the birds by air. In what has to be one of the most spectacularly woozy malfunctions ever to happen in the skies above the American Southwest, he found to his horror that when you toss Rhode Island Reds out of a small plane, well, let's just say the windblast hammers them in the most awful way, leaving lifeless chicken bodies scattered about the sagebrush. Jane too would be invited to do the optional chicken dance at the end of her course—her birds, though, having arrived by truck instead of airmail. She politely declined.

Outward Bound was founded in England during the onset of World War II, created by noted educator Kurt Hahn as a way to help sailors build the physical and mental skills they needed to increase their chances of survival if stranded at sea. It was hugely successful. Following the war, the program expanded to the United States, where it fell in fast with an idea popular off and on since the 1880s, which held that learning to be comfortable in unfamiliar, unpredictable environments did wonders for young people's self-esteem. Teens suffering from self-doubt, anger, or frustration, the thinking went, needed only to take the step of preparing themselves to be safe and comfortable in the wilderness. The wilderness would do the rest.

One of the things that shifted for Jane in Utah, something she never lost, was discovering that she had a talent for handling hardship. It was a quality underscored by a short quote mailed out to students before they even left for the course—three lines from *Zen and the Art of Motorcycle Maintenance* by Robert Pirsig. A guy, Jane reminded me, who had his own troubles with the whole sanity thing. "Physical discomfort is important only when the mood is wrong," she recited. "Then you fasten on to whatever thing is uncomfortable and call that the cause. But if the mood is right, then physical discomfort doesn't mean much."

What others saw as chores, or even as causes for anxiety— lumbering up steep inclines, setting up tarps in advance of fast-moving weather, cooking dinner on open fires—she treated with whispers of ceremony. As it happened, the presence required for Pirsig's "right mood" was what nature had been encouraging in Jane since her days as a Girl Scout leader: to be alert, to pay attention to changing circumstances. In Outward Bound she enjoyed an even bigger dose of the perspective she was learning to use to help with control issues—with the jagged disquiet that had driven her anorexia. In truth, she would never completely leave behind the unease she felt about what life might put in her lap, or in the laps of those she loved. For all her enchanting playfulness, she never wanted to be far from a plan, from a sense of structure. And yet what the wilderness kept giving her—part of the measure of sanity it offered—was the assurance that she could be strong in the face of random weather.

* * * *

I LAID THE BROWN POTTERY VASE IN THE TOP OF MY DAY PACK
and started walking from a set of corrals near the Notom Road—
heading west, toward Sheets Gulch and the stark, fluted edges of
the Waterpocket Fold. A cluster of cottonwoods was leafing out
along the wash, dripping with Jane's fleeting, electric green of
April. The skies were mostly clear, though in the west was a long
train of dark clouds, dragging their tails along the tops of the red
rock divide. Nature moves fast here, often violently, with storms
entirely out of sight sending walls of water pushing down slot
canyons, tearing boulders loose and ravaging the cottonwoods.
Yet another good reason to pay attention.

Fluttering on the ground that day were clusters of Apache
plume and rabbit brush, and along the damp edges of coulees,
the jointed stems of horsetail poked from the earth like bony
stalks of asparagus. The magpies were out in force, rising and
falling in ten- or twelve-foot dips, toying with the wind. I looked
halfheartedly for small landforms near big landforms, as per the
advice of the Hopi man, but had no real instinct for it. Still, in
the end I found myself on top of a small butte at the eastern edge
of the national park. The view whispered of a time scale so grand
as to be inconceivable: old swamps in what is now the tumble
of the Chinle Formation; massive desert dunes locked away in
Navajo Sandstone; the hiss of shallow seas, frozen in layers of
Mancos Shale.

The puffs of ash I spooned into the sky held together for a
long time on that strangely windless afternoon, drifting slowly to
the north against a reach of rust-colored sandstone. I placed the

spoon and jar in the sand at my feet. Then I lowered my body to the ground, laid my cheek against a warm slab of rock. A lone, pumpkin-shaped cloud drifted overhead, and dissolved. A hummingbird flew by on her way to grab lunch from a patch of star lilies, passing so close to my head that I could hear the whir of her wings. Just as happened in the Sawtooths, and again at that cabin in the southern Absarokas, for a precious few minutes there came a sense of putting the burden down. Like the hole in my life was getting smaller, a smear of black in a bigger world of sky and slickrock and morning glories. As if the magpies were carrying off some of the loss. As though the tiger beetles had loaded it onto their varnished backsides and were walking it out across the trackless sand.

* * * *

THE OLD PEOPLE OF THIS PLACE, THE PAIUTE, THOUGHT IT perfectly normal for beauty and chaos to stand together like this, hand in hand. Paiute creation myth tells how long ago, the earth was danced by two brothers, Coyote and Wolf. Wolf with his perfect, wholesome vision of the world, a creator who never wanted anything more than an abundant life for the people, a life free of anguish, free even of death. And the younger Coyote— spoiled, mischievous, a glib talker who time and again pulled his older brother away from any plans of perfection. After a time, Wolf went away, leaving the world to unfold according to the imaginations of Coyote. We cast our fate with Coyote, said the

Paiute. And so our lives are driven by this strange mix of sunlight and shadow, loveliness and fear.

When revisiting those kids from the wilderness therapy program I'd written about, I was heartened to find them mostly happy, content. With every one of them, I asked a question I'd asked ten years before: Why did that program work, when all the other interventions had failed? Their most frequent response was "It's the first place where what I did mattered."

The second most common remark: "It's where I finally experienced something beautiful."

The third: "It's the first time I ever felt spiritual," or "felt God," or "felt like I was a part of something bigger than just me."

Community. Beauty. Mystery.

WATER TO STONE, FIVE

Friday night, May 27. Search director Greg Brown calls to let us know they've found Jane's life jacket, sitting high and dry on a beach along the north shore of Obonga Lake, a half mile from the site of the wreck. A flash of hope. I tell Greg she'd be likely to sit on it, resting; in fact I'd seen her do it plenty of times, insulating herself from cold ground. Maybe she's hypothermic, I offer—some of the first signs of hypothermia being confusion and disorientation. Simply got up and walked away. The next morning, Tom, Martha, and I sit picking at plates of eggs in the hotel restaurant, weaving other scenarios, other flights of fancy that make her still alive.

Sensing we're going stir-crazy, Brad McCallum arranges for one of his officers to drive us back north, to the search site, figuring it will help us feel more connected to the rescue effort. When we arrive, Brown wastes no time pulling out maps and laptops, reviewing with us everything the search team has done over the past two and a half days. It strikes me that Jane would totally admire how organized he is, how capable. After an hour or so, the officer who drove us up from Thunder Bay asks if we'd like to get some lunch in Armstrong, about thirty miles north. It was where Jane and I had our last meal together: pizza in a well-lit little tavern on the main street of town. There was a television hanging from the ceiling above the bar, playing reruns of *America's Funniest Home Videos*.

We're out on the highway, ten miles north of the search command site, when a call comes over the radio. It's not an explicit exchange, and after signing off, the officer tells us Greg is asking us to return. It doesn't take two seconds for me to be swept into that maelstrom of dread I've been trying so hard to contain, ever since I stood at the flush pond and felt the wash of beautiful and goodbye. Everything's coming apart now. Back at the command center, I can see Greg Brown through the window of the car. The look on his face tells the end of the story.

"I'm afraid I have bad news," he says.

The next time I look up, having fallen to my knees in the sand, I see he's crying.

* * * *

THE SEARCHERS HAD COMBED THE BANKS OF THE KOPKA seven times in all. On the last try, one of the dogs stopped and pointed toward the river. The handler and his assistant looked, looked some more, but couldn't see anything in the dark, tannin-colored water. Just as they were about to move on, the assistant caught sight of something. They moved in closer, trying to study it from every angle; in the end, they decided it was fabric. Assembling the rest of the team, uncoiling rescue ropes, they managed a technical foray into the rapids. Finally, nearly three days to the hour after Jane disappeared, her body was pulled from the river.

* * * *

WHEN WORD GETS BACK TO THE CAFÉ IN RED LODGE, THE head cook, Nancy, takes a piece of chalk and writes a message on the blackboard that announces the daily specials, then hangs it so it faces the street: *We'll miss you, Sweet Jane.*

Word spreads fast. Soon after the café closes, at two in the afternoon, dozens of people start showing up at the restaurant, bringing heaping bowls of food, beginning a potluck that goes on late into the evening. So many stop Nancy and ask her what they can do to help that she has to invent tasks for them, the most common being to go pick flowers. By Sunday the place is all but covered in vases of daisies and roses and flag iris— filling the tables in the dining room, spilling across the window-sills and onto the tops of the reach-in coolers. For the next several days, every morning when the crew arrives to open the restaurant, they'll find more bouquets, more cards and prayer flags laid against the front door.

* * * *

BACK IN THUNDER BAY, SUNDAY IS A BLUR. THE ONLY POINT OF certainty was my obsession to drive Jane's ashes home in the van. To that end, Martha has been on the phone since just past dawn, calling the local officials who've been good enough to give us their home phone numbers. The coroner, for one, who as the last act of what began as a potential crime investigation will have to perform an autopsy. He offers to do this on his day off. The funeral director, Phil Medhurst, swings into action and makes arrangements for the cremation to happen the next morning.

Early Monday morning, I get out of bed and go knock on the door of Martha's room. When she opens it, I catch my breath. She's taken her long, thick brown hair, which for years had hung nearly to her waist, and cut it off in a ragged line at the top of her neck, using a pair of scissors borrowed from the hotel clerk in the middle of the night.

Tom leaves for the airport, to head back to Indiana, while Martha and I wait for the ashes to arrive at Blake's Funeral Home. We talk it over, decide to go down to the shore of Lake Superior for a parting ceremony—to Mariner Park, where the waters once held by the Kopka River pause for a time in the big lake before running on to the sea. The force of what's happened keeps growing, getting stronger, filling every muscle and fiber, making me weak in the knees, sick to my stomach. I know things are going to be this way for a long time. Like an avalanche that keeps running and running down the mountain, never exhausting itself, an endless, bitter cascade of ice and snow.

Down on the shore of Lake Superior I take the sock and sandal from my good foot and plant it in the lake, then lean over to wash my hands and face. Next I bring out a pack of Kool cigarettes that for years was stuffed into one of the food canisters in the van—a single cigarette being a small indulgence Jane enjoyed five or six times a year. Though neither Martha nor I smoke, we light one and pass it back and forth for several rounds, extinguish it, and then spread the remaining tobacco on the shore. Then Martha takes a paper towel from her daypack, unfolds it to reveal the hair she cut off back at the hotel in the middle of the night, bends over, and carefully lays it on the surface of the lake. It spreads out slowly, fanned by gentle waves, curling and twisting and then drifting out of sight.

On the way back to the van, Martha starts picking up every piece of trash she sees on the grounds of Mariner Park— something Jane did all the time. I hobble behind on my crutches, eager to help, snatching up bits of paper and cloth and the occasional cigarette butt and tossing them into nearby trash cans. When I crawl back into the passenger seat of the van, I notice wet spots on the chest of my shirt, from crying. Martha starts the engine. We both give a final look to the shore, and we drive away.

TO THE LAND OF
BEAR AND WOLF

.

Kenneth Rexroth, Carl Jung, Joseph Campbell—all of them bemoaned the loss of big myth in America, claiming it left us with withered imaginations. And that, in turn, caused a certain restless hunger—one that as often as not we ended up trying to stuff with consumer goods. Jung went so far as to claim there'd be no need for psychotherapy had we not turned our backs on story. I'd heard it all before. But by the second anniversary of Jane's death, I was also coming to believe that the power of those stories came largely from them putting us in touch with beauty, community, and mystery. And conversely, from tossing out hints about what can happen when such things disappear from our lives.

If I was going to have any chance of healing—if any of us were going to heal—we'd have to lay claim to a fresh trove of stories.

They'd have to be courageous stories—strong enough not only to help us see that the notion of being in control is the grandest of illusions, but at the same time teach us something about how to find calm in the eye of a storm. They'd have to be generous stories, compassionate enough to allow some measure of dignity toward "the other," be it the wolf hater or the wolf. And whatever tales we might spin about beauty would need to point back to the original Greek meaning of that word, which was to be of one's hour—be it the hour of a budding plant, as in youth, or the hour of the ripened fruit. And they'd have to be bold, audacious enough to remind us that when you're free from the feeling that something's lacking in your life, if instead you have real gratitude for what's actually there, then there's really no need to scour the countryside looking for hope.

* * * *

WITH YET ANOTHER SPRING RISING IN THE FOOTHILLS OF THE Rockies, I found myself putting out the welcome mat for an old desire: to get back to wilderness. Get back for real, not just for the scattering journeys. Jane herself would've no doubt prescribed for me a couple weeks out on open ground, waking up in some

GARY FERGUSON

honest-to-goodness middle of nowhere. I hooked up with a great friend, biologist Doug Smith, who'd gone to the Arctic with Jane and me on that canoe trip down the Hood River years before. He was happy to hear my cravings were coming back, happier still to stoke the fire. So we got down to plotting a trip back to the north country—this time to explore the remote lakes and streams near the headwaters of the mighty Thelon River in the Northwest Territories. Land of the bear and the wolf. We'd be just upwind from the magnificent twenty-thousand-square-mile Thelon Game Sanctuary, which among other things is homeland for the northern-most population of tundra-dwelling moose. And it was moose, said animal storytellers across thousands of years, which held clues to the mysterious fabric that binds life and death.

It was going to be the first time I'd been in a canoe since the wreck.

In the months before leaving, I was drawn to a curious perspective—a kind of psychic looking glass—one that I'd heard about years before when studying Aboriginal myths. The idea is that those of us who are still here, still walking around, are windows by which the ones who've passed on can still see, hear, taste, touch, and smell life on earth. Clearly, I had no foundation for such belief. Still, I decided to go back to the Far North determined to act like it was true. At one point, Doug offered that we could trade off between the bow and the stern of the boat, both of us typically being stern paddlers. I said I'd be okay in the bow, where Jane sat. Told him I wanted to feel the rivers and lakes the way she felt them: water parting around the hull in an easy hiss, the spray of breaking waves on my face and arms, the boat thudding under me as it drops hard into the troughs.

Unlike other trips to the Barren Lands, this was the first time we'd be going with a guide. But not just any guide. We'd be going with Alex Hall, a man who'd spent more days in the remote Canadian wilderness with a paddle than anyone alive. Joining us was a married pair of middle-aged biologists from New Hampshire, as well as Alex's oldest son, who in truth would've rather been wandering the Edmonton Mall than out in the wilderness. With us too was Monte Hummel of the World Wildlife Fund—arguably among the most capable, effective conservationists on the continent. Like us, Hummel wasn't there just to canoe. He was there to canoe with Alex Hall.

In 1971, with a freshly signed master's degree in wildlife biology in his pocket, Hall and a buddy had left Ontario for the heart of nowhere, driving more than three thousand miles to the far-flung outpost of Yellowknife. From there they'd hopped on a float-plane with a canoe strapped on it and begun a thirty-seven-day trip down the Thelon and Hanbury rivers to Baker Lake, becoming only the eleventh recreational party to make that journey.

Later, finding himself going stir-crazy at a desk job in Ottawa as an environmental consultant, he had decided to go west for good, to create his own business as a canoe guide in the Barren Lands. The next summer he was back on the tundra with boat and paddle, launching an eleven-week, 1,150-mile canoe odyssey across the mainland Northwest Territories on seven different rivers, from the Saskatchewan border to the Arctic coast.

The government officials in Yellowknife in charge of issuing business permits had been skeptical of the guiding idea. With good reason. The whole of the summer of 1974, Hall had one client. The following year, he had another one.

"I'm stubborn," he told me. "I kept the faith."

He'd also kept paddling, along the way becoming the first human to float a long list of rivers and watersheds. To this day, some of the routes he discovered remain known only to him, making him very protective of the region. By 1979 his trips were fully booked. Which has pretty much been the case for thirty years.

* * * *

WE NEEDED TWO FLOATPLANES OUT OF FORT SMITH, EACH loaded with meticulous attention to detail: Duluth packs and tents and paddles and cook stoves precisely placed, the center thwarts of the canoes removed so the shells of the boats could be nestled like cups and strapped to the floats of the planes. Bush planes are noisy, not good for conversation, so on the outbound journey we mostly stared out the windows—looking at landscapes vast and empty beyond imagining. The clusters of birch and spruce trees near Fort Smith grew smaller and smaller, then all but faded, yielding thousands of square miles of open tundra broken by lakes and ponds, by chains of side channels and bogs flashing in the sun. And then the polygons: mysterious earthen clusters of perfect geometric-shaped pockets fifty to seventy feet across, each framed by high walls of earth pushed up by the underlying ice, joined to the others in what from the air look like massive honeycombs. And at the bottom of each one, a pocket of cold water the color of sky.

Touching down on Lake Terry around eleven in the morning, the pilots maneuvered the leading edges of the floats onto a sandy beach, and we hurried to off-load equipment. When the planes took off again, the drones of their engines finally fading to the south, all eyes tuned to Alex. He stood tall and lanky—dressed mostly in wool, looking a lot like a guy from a 1960s issue of *Outdoor Life*. There was the obligatory bathroom talk, reviewing the dos and don'ts of crapping on the tundra. He brought out different pieces of equipment, then launched us in a practice session setting up his tents. He struck me as looking much younger than his sixty-seven years, in part because of the economy of his movement, smooth and efficient in that way of men and women who spend big blocks of time traveling through wild places. Even his conversations were economical, measuring out his points and opinions, even his stories, in a manner simple and steady and clear.

Now and then there came the trace of a smile to Hall's face, mostly when he was off alone, pausing with hand on hip, staring across the tundra. It's hard to fathom the memories he carried: Climbing some high hill, untold miles from anyone, and finding caribou as far as the eye can see—a hundred thousand, two hundred thousand animals—moving past hour after hour, for the better part of a day. Or the countless encounters he'd had with tundra wolves. Or the dozens of times he'd slipped silently past eight-hundred-pound grizzlies feeding on the shore.

After forty years traveling by canoe, Hall had his systems down: packing, portaging, cooking, setting up camp. He declined every one of our offers to help with chores—not because we were guests, but because after four decades of outfitting, he knew damn well it took less energy to do things himself. Which left us just one task we could pour our team spirit into—portaging. And in that we shined. Everyone tackled the job with gusto, hauling canoes and paddles and heavy Duluth packs out of one watershed and into the next, sometimes a mile or more away, one trip over and back and then another, then still another. Maybe because he'd had plenty of guests who were all too happy to leave the heavy lifting to him, on most days he complimented us on a job well done. It left us feeling like little kids who'd just pleased the teacher.

On the first afternoon, as we were going through the dry run of setting up the tents he'd supplied, Doug and I managed to break a framing pole. Right away we got panicked looks on our faces, wondering which one of us would draw the short straw and go confess. I lost. Later in the day, when food bags were being handed out to individual boats, we got the heaviest one of all, which we named "the pig." Each of the bags was numbered according to which one was opened on a particular day, and the pig had the highest number of all. Which meant we'd be portaging it every day until the end of the trip. We told each other it wasn't any sort of punishment for busting the tent pole. Just a sign of how tough Alex thought we were.

During one of our walkabouts outside camp, I happened to hear Alex and Monte Hummel talking about cloudberries, a ground fruit found only on the world's northern tundra. Monte thought it tasted like a cross between a strawberry and an apricot, talking about it with that dreamy look people have when they're recalling the best meal of their lives. "There could be a few left," Alex said, then he described what to look for. "But it's probably too late in the year."

From that day on I became consumed by thoughts of finding cloudberries. Tasting cloudberries. Though I looked every day, at every lunch stop and at every camp, I couldn't find even one. And I started thinking I'd have to come back just for this.

* * * *

I'D WONDERED MANY TIMES WHAT IT WOULD BE LIKE TO SLIP into a canoe and start paddling again. The feel of my fingers around the shaft of the paddle, the smell of lake water—would all that be a comfort or a trigger, hurtling me back to that awful morning on the Kopka? Maybe because I was doing it with a good friend, maybe because of the wild thrum of the north country, maybe because I knew Jane would want me here, it felt exactly right. Like the unclenching of fists after a bout of anger, like a long, slow exhale. We started on open water stirred by a mild breeze, which kept noodling soothing rhythms of waves against the hull. Doug and I chatted as we paddled, speculating about the weather, pulling out binoculars every few minutes, pointing them toward distant sharp-shinned hawks and Arctic terns and horned grebes and eiders and canvasbacks and buffleheads.

The second day ushered in an unbroken string of foul weather, wind and cold and heavy rain across most of eleven days, drearier than even Alex Hall had ever seen. At one point, at the edge of an enormous lake, our group ended up huddled on a high promontory against a ferocious wind, maps splattered across the rocks, trying to gauge whether we could make a safe crossing on a big stretch of water churning with whitecaps. In the end we decided to go for it, hugging the shore hour after hour, all the while buckets of cold spray piling over the bow of the boat and wetting my face and hands. Even then, as well as under every leaden sky still to come, I was more deeply content than I'd been in a long while. I missed Jane. Wished she were there with me on that cold water, afloat in that boundless world. But there were no flashbacks of the Kopka. No thought that I shouldn't be paddling again, no wish to be anywhere else. I couldn't know if Jane was somehow privy to the touch and smell and throttle of that rain and wind, as those old Aboriginal stories suggested. What mattered is that I'd taken the chance to offer it. By imagining that I was opening up for her benefit, giving her access to smell and sound and taste and feeling, what I'd done was allow my own reentry into the physical world.

As was true years before, on the Hood River, the evenings

were priceless—most of them spent along some beautiful stretch of sand esker—massive blond dunes that stretch across much of the Far North. After setting up our tent, Doug and I would split from the group for an hour or so, measure out our allotted drams of the Scotch we'd packed in, fire up cigars, and talk. Talk about being with Jane on the Hood River. About how early on, Doug had taught her to chew tobacco—and how to his astonishment she had gone with it, sharing pinches of Skoal with him down a hundred miles of river. We talked about how she liked to get up early in the morning and pass out strong coffee. How at the end of the trip we'd all stripped off our clothes and run nearly naked into the cold waters of the Arctic Sound.

During one such conversation, far out on the water, began the first of what became many days of loon song. I told Doug that for me, the bird was forever linked to the Kopka. I told how, not long after Jane's death, still baffled by the pair of loons appearing on the flush pond below the rapids—overcome by the message "beautiful" and "goodbye"—I started poking through stories told of the birds by the Ojibwa people residing in that part of Canada. They describe them as couriers between earth and the hereafter, assigned the job of passing messages between the living and the dead. What I didn't say is that now, whenever one lets loose in the northern twilight, when a pair starts trading yodels across the cold waters of some unnamed lake, I listen with all my might. But there are no more messages. Just the usual wild cacophony— that strange, rolling peal of crying and laughing.

* * * *

OUR FINAL CAMP OF THE TRIP WAS A SUN-SPLASHED EVENING
along the edge of an enormous sand esker, uncurling into lake
water the color of the tropics. Everyone joined Alex on a long
ramble across the tundra, looking for a certain wolf den he knew
about, then climbing the high ridges and glassing for caribou.
In mid-afternoon a small herd of musk oxen appeared in a draw
some two miles away, and the group decided to hike over for a
closer look.

Doug and I made a circuitous amble back to camp, there
settling in for a long nap on the thick mats of caribou lichen that
blanketed the spruce forest. All day long I'd been noticing how
odd the plant growth is in the Barren Lands. The same basic species that in Montana or Colorado are spread across thousands of
vertical feet, on the tundra get squeezed into a few yards. Here
we could stand in a moist, lush pocket of heather, and in three
steps up a tiny rise find ourselves in a world populated by lichens,
the undisputed masters of earth's driest lands.

Then, close to camp, I saw it: the fabled cloudberry. Though
a little past prime, the fruits—roughly the color of peach jam—
were still swollen with juice. I popped a couple in my mouth.
There it was, the promised nectar of strawberries and apri-
cots. With the sky washed in the final breath of summer, once
again Doug and I split from the group, poured our final drams
of Scotch, and talked of big things. I told him about those old
story prompts: beauty, community, and mystery. Also about how

the kids in wilderness therapy, knowing nothing about any of that, listed the very same things as part of what allowed them to finally kick heroin, quit stealing, stop cutting themselves. It had been beauty, community, and mystery that opened them to the really important things in their lives—things that had been stuck inside, desperate to come out.

"So look," he said. "What if society's moving too fast? What if we're too distracted for any of that—the beauty and the mystery?"

Then he took his last swallow of Scotch, snubbed out his cigar in the sand.

"And if we've really forgotten, what could make us remember?"

WATER TO STONE, SIX

The memorial service was held on June 10, three days after the surgery on my broken leg, in the Catholic church in Red Lodge. Other than the Civic Center, it was the building in town that held the most people. I lurched through the side door of the church on my crutches, my brother at my side—him looking nervous, as if he thought I was about to do a head plant. Inside the sanctuary, some six hundred people were waiting, friends and family from all over the country. The mere sight of them started me blubbering.

I'd asked for room in the service for people to tell stories, and they came in good measure. Funny tales. Lovely ones, too.

When it was my turn, I explained how Jane often remarked that when it came her time to go, she hoped the end would come in a wild place, doing what she loved. And so it did. Somehow though, I said, I imagined the end being decades away. Maybe with her as an old woman out on some last camping trip, snugged in a down bag, staring out the door flap of the tent into a sky riddled with stars.

I told them too about how a week before the accident, on a lonely highway in southern Canada, in the middle of a game we sometimes played where we tried to imagine what it would be like to live in other places, Jane had said finding another community no longer seemed an option. "I couldn't quit the people."

Two musician friends agreed to sing a song for the service. It was Judy Collins's "Since You've Asked"—the tune I first played for her driving through the Sawtooth Valley in my '64 Pontiac Tempest, and later, the one I had that musician play for her in Michigan, on the day I asked her to marry me.

The Red Lodge Fire Department, which included most of Jane's fellow EMT and search-and-rescue workers, had parked their biggest fire truck outside the church, the ladder raised in tribute. Near the end of the service the dispatcher issued a so-called "final page"—an honor given to those who have died in the line of duty, or who have made significant contributions to the community.

The radio crackled: "Red Lodge Fire and Rescue, Dispatch." Then a few long seconds of quiet, a gentle woosh of static.

"This is a final page for Jane Ferguson. She died in the

wilderness, doing what she loved. Her dedication and compassion for her fellow citizens will not soon be forgotten."

And then, "Dispatch clear." For about a minute afterward it was completely quiet; the whole place seemed ready to collapse into sobs.

Jane's brother Tom had an idea to give away young trees to the mourners. So after returning from Canada we contacted the state nursery in Missoula, bought 350 little blue spruce trees, then handed them out to people as they left the church. Even now I'm stopped on the sidewalk once or twice a month by someone wanting to update me on the current height and general well-being of their "Jane tree." One of her search-and-rescue partners, on moving to a new house two years after her death, dug up his Jane tree and replanted it in the yard of his new home. Another friend looked me up in December 2011, eager to tell me that his Jane tree was finally big enough to hold a string of Christmas lights.

Long before the accident, Jane wrote in her will that on her death, she wanted a party. So after the service, several hundred of us walked the five blocks from the Catholic church to the backyard of the café. The local brewer was there with his beer trailer, and for the next several hours people from all over the country spilled into the gardens with glasses of ale, talking and laughing and crying, telling story after story, a lot of them ones I'd never heard. I tried hard to hold on to those stories, wanting so badly to remember. But most of them lingered just for a minute or two, then slipped away on the June breeze.

THE WILD WE'VE
FORGOTTEN

W hat was it that left America so incredibly eager to eat up the antics of Joe Knowles—the guy who in 1913 stripped down to a G-string and ran off to live for two months as a wild man? What cravings launched a land-preservation movement the likes of which the world had never seen, creating a flurry of outdoor youth groups from coast to coast, from the Sons of Daniel Boone to the Boy Pioneers? Igniting a profusion of school gardens, and stoking into full-blown holiday status a celebration started in the 1890s called Bird Day, uncannily similar to today's Earth Day?

Beyond the Puritans, who mostly saw the devil behind every tree, a lot of newcomers arriving to the continent in the 1600s rushed into wild America with open arms, mythologizing it at every turn. Part of their enthusiasm had to do with a renaissance going on in both Europe and Great Britain, a casting off of a church-driven orthodoxy that had held nature at arm's length, making it malicious and malevolent for a thousand years. For centuries the Catholic Church had offered a loosely woven tale about earth having been created in a kind of smooth symmetry, what was sometimes called a "mundane egg." Then humans sinned, the story went, the flood came, and when the water receded again, there were all sorts of irregular landforms—crumpled mountains, rugged coastlines. All of which were said to serve as reminders that humans are inherently evil.

By the sixteenth and seventeenth centuries, though, fresh air had started to blow across the Western world. It came from poets like Milton and Denham. And from science, too, where guys like Galileo were making all kinds of fascinating discoveries about the natural world (including the fact that there were mountains on the moon, which left pundits wondering why God would plant reminders of our evil natures in places where no one could even see them). For many merchants and traders, coming to North America felt like crawling out into the bright sunlight, after having spent a very long time in a dimly lit cave.

French trappers, for instance, traded story images with nearby tribes the way beads got swapped for beaver pelts. The newcomers routinely borrowed pieces of indigenous creation stories, especially those with mysterious nature spirits, weaving them into hybrid tales of their own. Early in the nineteenth century, poet Rodman Drake penned a long verse called *The Culprit Fay*, said to be the first great work of American literature—a work *American Monthly Magazine* called "one of the most exquisite productions in the English language." The tale was crafted around the Iroquois "Pukwudgies," or little vanishers, setting them against a curious mix of Arthurian legend and Celtic mysticism.

And that was just the beginning. By the mid-1700s, wild nature was being called "the great equalizer," a homage to the fact that it handed out its blessings and risks equally, no matter the money in your pocket or the blue in your blood. Which explains why nature was the stewpot of choice for gathering symbols of an emerging democracy. In one of the first skirmishes of the Revolutionary War, off the coast of Maine, the townspeople of Machias took off after a British Navy crew commandeering a shipload of pine, chased it down, captured it, decorated it with pine boughs, and called it Liberty. We Americans pretty much always saw ourselves in terms of nature—plastering it on our state flags, stamping it into our coins, sewing it across panels of the quilts we pulled over us to keep warm at night.

Some predicted the United States would produce more artists, more creative people of every stripe, simply because we were spending so much time rubbing elbows with the woods. Later, nineteenth-century superstar pundit Henry George told his readers that "The free, independent spirit, the energy and hopefulness that have marked our people are not causes, but results. They have sprung from unfenced land. Public domain has given a consciousness of freedom even to the dweller in crowded cities, and has been a wellspring of hope even to those who have never thought of taking refuge upon it." Never mind if you didn't actually make it to the big wilds. Just knowing they were out there would engender a "consciousness of freedom." *Scientific American* editor Gerard Peil was still ringing the same bell in the 1950s, claiming the highest value of wilderness was to "remind us of a just society."

There'd also been a deep, abiding grassroots movement in the country to link unfettered landscapes to spirituality. The Hudson River School artists—arguably the most influential artistic movement in our history—turned first to the unsullied landscapes of New England and later to the West, promoting the idea that such places allowed nothing less than the direct experience of God.

"We may not go to church as often as our forefathers," celebrated naturalist John Burroughs said. "But we go to the woods much more."

This too, then, is where we've come from. Who we are. And no amount of hating wolves or pushing to sell off the public lands by the Sagebrush Rebels, no amount of weary disillusionment or forgetting by the baby boomers, can ever take it away.

THE CARRY HOME

A t around fourteen I started keeping a record of sorts, a
journal, scribbling into spiral notebooks I got for 59¢ at
Brite-Way, the same ones our parents bought my brother and
me every fall for school. A couple years after Jane died, I pulled
them out again. The thing I noticed was one big theme spilling across those narrow-ruled lines—an attempt to shore up this
barely controlled passion I had for moving into the bigger world,
out into nature. Maybe it was anxious hunger to be gone from
the house in the face of the beatings. Or maybe it was some kind
of defense against kids who thought me strange, poking fun at
me in the school newspaper for this great plan I'd blabbed to

someone about riding my bike 1,500 miles to the mountains of Colorado. I had a primal knot in my stomach whenever I read some line like Thoreau's "the mass of men lead lives of quiet desperation," or Oliver Wendell Holmes talking about "those that never sing, but die with all their music in them." I missed no chance to add my own thoughts on the topic, writing insipid little poems, like this one, penned at fourteen with a blue ballpoint:

The old man's eyes were tearful,
As he journeyed back the years
A once hopeful life now silenced, from decades filled with fears.
The island that he sailed for, is the same we all must reach,
But in the journey lies the treasure, and not upon the beach.

I wrote lots of pep talks to myself. And most curious of all is that so much of that encouragement held the feeling that at some point in the future, I would find myself lost. I'd be in great need of ferocious trust. "Never lose sight of this fire!" I wrote. And "The passion will save you!"

And sure enough, that last week of May in 2005, when our Old Town canoe flipped in the Kopka and Jane was gone forever, much of my passion went with her, to the bottom of that cold river. For a long time I was pretty sure I'd never trust again. But things were beginning to stir. Back home again from that canoe trip with Doug to the Thelon River, I was seeing things again: Canada geese dropping onto the waters of Rock Creek after a thousand miles of flying. Thousand-pound moose easing through the aspen trees without a sound. Life was flashing again—fresh, coming and going on the in-betweens.

* * * *

ONE DAY IN MARCH 2009, I WAS TEN MILES UP THE CANYON AT a certain mountain spring we locals are especially fond of— beside the tiny flow pipe, I tipped a metal cup to my lips and swallowed the frost of it. Standing there, smelling conifer sap in the air, thinking really of nothing at all, I was suddenly struck by a thought that the time had come to make the final two scat- terings. Furthermore, that they'd consist of a single trek by foot: walking just over sixty miles from the front door of my house into the Absaroka-Beartooth Wilderness, where I'd make the first scattering at a favorite alpine lake, and then on for forty miles more, for the final ceremony, in a spectacular valley in the northeast corner of Yellowstone National Park. The certainty of that idea, the way it arrived fully formed in my mind, points to a curious quality of grief journeys. The initial shock and terror of losing Jane were followed by a sense of the world being com- pletely shattered, busted to pieces. Coming back to life required a kind of reassembly. Which was a task that took a good deal more focus, more attention, than I tended to give to daily life. In that attentive state, free of distractions, I got quiet enough to hear my intuition. And more often than not, it was remarkably reliable.

I drove home from the spring, pulled out the appropriate topo maps, spread them out on the dining room table, started figuring the route. The journey would start with a sharp ascent, climbing more than five thousand feet to Line Creek Plateau, and from there head southeast for two days toward the high, wild edges of northwest Wyoming. That part of the trek, at least, would be a carbon copy of a 140-mile hike I had made to write *Hawks Rest*, living for three months in what geographers consider the most remote location in the lower 48. On that journey I'd left my front door with sixty-eight-year-old LaVoy Tolbert, the former education director at the wilderness therapy program I'd written about.

Lavoy and I departed just a couple months after Jane had called it quits at both Outward Bound and the Park Service, trading in her backpack and ranger duds to help start the fresh food café in Red Lodge. After a decade being away six months a year, either on the trail or in Yellowstone, she wanted to spend time closer to home. Yet for all her enthusiasm—and for Jane, enthusiasm was never in short supply—it was anything but easy to go from earning a living in some of the wildest places in America to showing up each day at a restaurant at five in the morning to serve cage-free eggs. Plain and simple, she was missing wild country. To quench her thirst, she decided to come along with LaVoy and me for a while, joining us for four days of our eleven-day walk to Hawks Rest, hiking with us for about sixty miles, from the Clarks Fork Valley to Yellowstone Lake.

We'd crossed a remote stream called Papoose Creek, and shortly afterward the trail began to braid, winding up the canyon across increasingly steep slopes of crumbling soil, finally petering out altogether. From then on we had to make our way west by means of spotty elk trails, steering toward a saddle at the east edge of the national park, some three miles away. In time, though, even the elk trails deteriorated, most washed away by floods, leaving us to head upstream along high, steep banks of loose volcanic soil, capped by rugged cliffs. LaVoy and I decided to stay lower down, moving ahead like a couple of over-the-hill Tarzans, literally swinging forward in the worst places by grabbing onto branches of lodgepole pines. Jane, meanwhile, sought a route higher up the slope. Halfway across she found herself trapped, stuck high above the creek on a two-inch ledge of rock. Unable to move in either direction, she freed herself of her pack, letting it slide down the slope into a downed log, where I scrambled to retrieve it.

No sooner had I reached the pack when out of the corner of my eye, I caught sight of her sliding down the hill at terrific speed, careening toward a giant fallen log spiked its entire length with stout, broken branches. I lunged to catch her, but there was no time. By some miracle, her slide ended in one of the very few spots on the trunk free of broken branches; there were cuts on her hands and arms, a nasty bruise on her thigh, but nothing worse. We were all shaken, knowing full well she'd nearly suffered a serious, even fatal puncture wound. She stood for a while by the creek, alone, running it all through her head, being hard on herself. She could've waded the creek or gone higher, onto the more solid footing of the upper cliffs.

When we finally got to Boot Jack Gap that night, we were

exhausted. Over dinner, the sour taste of Jane's slide almost washed away, she turned philosophical.

"I just figured out why it's so important for me to be out here again," she told us. "I need to feel vulnerable."

She said her life had become safe, and as far as she was concerned, her best days had always been at the edge of her comfort zone. Not that she thought the accident was a good thing. But it pushed her across a threshold of sorts. It left her with an intense sense of presence. The kind she used to tell me was a part of feeling alive.

* * * *

ON THIS TRIP TO SCATTER HER ASHES, I'D BE TAKING ON COMpany of a rather different sort. I'd been writing for the *Los Angeles Times*, mostly working with Tom Curwen—one of those rare journalists still headlong in love with language and image—a perfectionist nearly to a fault, animated by and beholden to the simple thrill of a story well and honestly told. When he heard of my plans to walk to Yellowstone, he tiptoed onto terribly awkward ground, asking if he might witness some of it for a story he envisioned writing. At first I quietly rejected the idea out of hand, thinking this was best left a private affair. But I told him I'd think about it. A week or so later it struck me that if anyone was capable of squeezing something useful from all of this, Tom would be the guy to pull it off.

He showed up in mid-August, arriving with photographer

Brian Van Der Brug, who'd barely had time to repack for Montana after returning from assignment in Iraq. We kicked things off with beer at the local brewery, which featured the added attraction of a men's bathroom wallpapered with topographical maps of the entire Absaroka-Beartooth Wilderness. Standing at the sink, we could see our journey from start to finish, stretching roughly from the toilet stall all the way to the hand dryer. Next it was back to my house, where we laid out mounds of gear and dehydrated food on the floor of my garage, sorting and stuffing it into backpacks.

* * * *

WE WALKED OUT THE FRONT DOOR EARLY ON THE MORNING OF August 21, strolling into the well-buttered light of full summer. One last time, then, for the brown pottery jar with Jane's ashes, riding again in the top of my pack, cushioned by a stack of topo maps and a small nest of foul-weather gear. After two hundred yards of aspen forest we reached Highway 212, then headed south for three miles to a packed dirt road on the east side of Rock Creek. Then another three-quarters of a mile to the Mount Maurice trailhead. The sky was flawless, and in the cool of morning the air was thick with the peppery scent of pine. Perfect day, I said to Tom, for the beginning of this end.

Knowing how tough the first day of hiking would be for us, Rand—the old friend who made the box that holds Jane's ashes—had offered to haul our backpacks to the plateau with his faithful mule Sadie and his horse Sparhawk. Under that scenario we would have the great luxury of pushing up five thousand feet wearing only day packs. Rand's kindness reminded me how, four years ago, in the weeks following Jane's death, the people carrying soup and casseroles and tamales into my kitchen, unpacking my van and cleaning my house and mowing my lawn, weren't just being good to me. Jane was also lost to them, and helping out was a way they brought service to their own terrible grief. So in the end I accepted Rand's offer. Like all good journalists, Tom and Brian tried hard to keep their reactions to my choice close to the vest; still, the idea of a mule shuttle seemed to leave them more than a little pleased.

It wasn't easy backpacking next to a reporter, especially a good one, not to mention a photographer who routinely hovers and spins in all manner of crazy gyrations, struggling for the best angle with which to capture some essence of the passage. At first, there were stray moments when I found myself second-guessing the decision to let them come along. It was frustrating when I asked their opinions about campsites or lunch stops and they told me they didn't care, that this was my journey. One of the essential pleasures of being in the backcountry with other people, after all, is the camaraderie of choices. But day after day, living in the wild would loosen them. There'd be something about our raising small swallows of whiskey in the last of the alpenglow. Something in making snide remarks about Brian snoring in his tent a few feet away; in eating beans and farting like men do in the backcountry, farting being among the most reliable means of letting your inner ten-year-old out of the closet. Those things would close the gap.

We reached Line Creek Plateau at half past noon, twenty thousand steps or so, across ten miles. There we found Rand bedecked in his trail gear—cowboy hat and leather chaps and gloves—kicking back with Sadie and Sparhawk in the shade of a small cluster of whitebark pine. Being an accomplished packer, he was set on making a quick turnaround, wanting to play his trip as the wilderness always suggests such trips should be played, especially with animals in tow, allowing plenty of time for mishaps on the journey home. After a quick visit, we sent him off with thanks and good wishes, told him we'd see him again in four days, for the scattering at Becker Lake.

After he left, we stood for a time at the edge of the tundra. Rock Creek was a thin flashing line four thousand feet below, a twist of fast water pushing out of the high country toward open prairie. Directly opposite, at roughly the same elevation, beyond the glacial valley that cradles Rock Creek, was Hell Roaring Plateau—a seventeen-mile-long run of nut-brown tundra rising in a cockeyed ramp toward some of the most massive, broad-shouldered peaks anywhere in the northern Rockies.

Whatever poetry there may be in the Beartooths, on a lot of days it's less meter and rhyme than feral free verse. Only now and then does Robert Browning's rosy earth show itself, his lovely, bucolic dew-pearled hillsides. Just as often it's Gary Snyder—"ice-scratched slabs and bent trees, weathering land, wheeling sky." Here avalanches run like thunder, while boulders big as school busses let loose in sudden leaps for the valley floor. Here wolves pad across the snow, and in May, grizzlies amble across the elk calving grounds, walking fixed patterns through the loose bunches of sage, looking for newborns. In autumn, moose wander through the valley bottoms, the bulls made crazy by the mating rut, casting aggravated looks at passersby, trying to decide whether to let them pass or stomp them into the ground.

Except for the early trappers, Anglos showed up here in the latter half of the nineteenth century, mostly in service of other Anglos with appetites for profit. Among the first was a clutch arriving in July of 1898: A rough and ready Norwegian photographer named Anders Wilse. A couple of engineers. A handful of properly bearded, fly-bitten hunters and horse packers. In charge was mineralogist James Kimball, a wad of Rockefeller's money in his pocket, readying to launch the first honest-to-goodness exploration of what a century later Jane and I would come to call the home mountains.

Twenty years before Kimball, a geologist by the name of William Holmes had been in the area, part of a survey team in Yellowstone. But his reports were filled with errors, suggesting he'd probably taken only the most casual look at the Beartooths and made up the rest. Four years later, General Philip Sheridan— famous for battering the Plains Indians onto reservations— marched out of the northeast corner of Yellowstone into this same high country, moving down Line Creek Plateau and on out to the Yellowstone River. But he too was, for the most part, just passing through. Which is how Kimball and his boys became the first serious chroniclers of this place. Their spirits were up. The last half of summer sprawled out like a good dream. At their first camp, just outside Cooke City, talk around the campfire was loud and full of bluster.

It snowed and sleeted every week that summer. The wind blew so hard it knocked down tents and sent stovepipes flying across the tundra. After checking with locals for details about the central Beartooths and getting nothing, the party made their way to Kersey Lake, and from there began forays to Island Lake, to the headwaters of the Clarks Fork, and finally up to the summit of Mount Dewey, achieving that only after being turned back time and again by bone-numbing rain and gale-force winds. All the while they were mapping, recording elevations. And most important of all—at least to Rockefeller and the Rocky Fork Coal Company—they were keeping an eye out for precious minerals.

On it went, week after week, setting up base camps and making wind-blasted day trips into the unknown, the journeys broken by occasional dashes back to Cooke City for more supplies. Kimball's descriptions of the place are a mix of eager scientific jargon—waxing on about porphyrite dykes and feldspathic granite—and little-boy amazement at the steep gorges choked with rocks, ice-gouged lake basins, waterfalls by the dozen. And always the "treacherous weather—pelting hailstorms, bleak winds," including a bivouac at Goose Lake that would leave him for years afterward referring to the place as Camp Misery.

The snows came early that year, pushing Kimball and a

couple frostbitten cohorts to lower elevations near Red Lodge. Amazingly, after a brief rest, a small party attempted still more forays in and around the Beartooths, wandering the mountains off and on all through October. They clambered over Dead Indian Pass Road, noting how the sides of the route were piled with "snubbing" logs—cut trees tied by travelers to the backs of their wagons in order to keep them from careening out of control on the two-thousand-foot, mile-and-a-half-long descent. Coming to the edge of the Absarokas, they discovered the trails already buried in snow. From there it was back around the Beartooths to the East Rosebud, where on the first night of their arrival Kimball watched in horror as eighty-mile-an-hour winds destroyed his twelve-by-sixteen-foot wall tent, tearing the eyelets out of the fabric and sending clothes, bedding, even the woodstove flying. "Everything had soared away, except blankets under the weight of their possessors. Minor articles, usually worn in pairs, never found their mates. No further adventure proved necessary to force the conviction that endurable conditions for camp life had come to an end for the season."

It will take Tom, Brian, and me two days of walking the land Kimball mapped, heading south and west, to reach the end of the Line Creek Plateau. Then we'll turn north, toward the heart of those distant peaks. Standing on Line Creek Plateau that day, looking into that wild maze of uplands, seeing what we'd be crossing, from the looks on their faces my traveling companions seemed to be wondering about the general soundness of my plan. Maybe they were imaging some sort of Kimball-style expedition.

Days later, they'll confess that back in their hotel rooms in Red Lodge, they pulled out their maps and formed a secret exit strategy, on the off chance they'd signed on with a crazy man.

* * * *

OUR FIRST CAMP WAS HIGH ON THE TUNDRA, IN A NARROW saddle, fifteen miles from my house. All of Wyoming was stretching out along the southern horizon, while a sprawling slice of Montana unfolded to the north. From that plateau, horizon to horizon, the entire world felt like a scrapbook of the treks Jane and I had made, long ones and short ones and in-between ones, in every season. Forty miles to the southeast were autumn rambles along the summits of the Pryors. Fifty miles to the northwest, ski trips into the Crazy Mountains. A hundred miles east, spring trips by canoe down the Yellowstone River, riots of Canada geese chattering in our wake.

Except for a herd of meandering elk cows and calves, Tom, Brian, and I were all alone. As far as we knew, there wasn't another traveler for miles. And it would be that way for nearly the entire trip. Still, standing on the south edge of the tundra after dark, pissing one last time before bed, my companions seemed disappointed to look over the edge and see the lights of Clark, Wyoming, thousands of feet below. What they didn't know was that this was the last of it. For the next nine nights, there'd be only empty meadows and black piney woods. Even the moon was absent for the following six days, at which point the new crescent peeled back to cast light again on a steep and tumbled sea of granite ridges and domes.

Our first morning in the backcountry was bright, cool. The wind pushed and poked as we meandered across some nine miles of tundra near 9,500 feet, mostly without the benefit of trails. As was true the day before, on the far northwest horizon we could see the high shoulders of Lone Mountain, a cone-shaped mass of granite rising above a great upheaval of tundra, marking a spot near where friends would gather with us for the first of these two final scattering ceremonies. Step by step, we were moving into serious grizzly country. Each of us in turn would rouse from the tent in the wee hours and stumble out into the cold to take a leak, all the while steering our headlamps in nervous sweeps through the darkness, looking for the flash of eyes looking back.

The idea of grizzlies proved to be the one thing powerful enough to make Tom pause from questioning me about the canoe wreck on the Kopka. He was clearly nervous about them, shouting, "Hey bear!" at regular intervals to announce his presence, even on open tundra where it was possible to see for miles. We broke early afternoon in a meadow of forget-me-nots; I slipped off my pack, pointed toward Yellowstone, told him one of my favorite bear stories.

One night Jane and I were bedded down on the east side of Rampart Pass—the third of six nights out, walking from Togwotee Pass to Cody—in the thick of the grizzly-rich southern reaches of the Absaroka Range. Dawn was just breaking when suddenly I bolted awake to the one sound you never want to hear outside your tent. Something close to a grunting pig. Which I wished with every fiber of my being was in fact a grunting pig. Carefully peaking out the screen door, I spotted a big male grizzly not six feet away, ripping apart dead logs and snapping up ants and grubs, groaning and mumbling to himself in what seemed a coarse imitation of a good purr.

Jane was still asleep, so I gently woke her; with my face close to hers I put my index finger against my lips, signaling the need for quiet. She rolled over in her bag toward the screen door, spotted the bear, then after watching him for a couple of minutes turned back to face the ceiling of the tent. By now I was totally shot through with adrenaline, eyes wide, my right hand tightly clutched around a can of bear spray. Time was going very, very slowly. After another ten minutes, my whole body buzzing, I looked over to check on Jane to see how she was handling the stress. Fast asleep. After what seemed an excruciatingly long time, the bear finally moseyed off. Slowly but surely I settled down, started breathing normally again. Jane woke up a little while after that, said she was hungry for oatmeal.

* * * *

ON THE SECOND DAY OF THE SCATTERING JOURNEY WE COVered just over eleven miles, the last of them rough—up and over a steep, narrow pass high on the tundra, then a scramble on weary legs across a long run of talus, finally descending in the twilight to a mosquito-infested bottom just downstream from Christmas

Lake. The next morning I pulled out the map and compass to triangulate a bearing toward a major trail we'd need to intersect to the west. We crossed Littlerock Creek, and once again started climbing toward the sky.

Barely an hour went by that Tom wasn't peppering me with questions. "What were you thinking in those minutes following the wreck?" "Where were you when they found Jane's body?" Yet the farther we went, the less the questions cut me. Even when I did break down, when I tried to tell Tom what this place meant to us over eighteen years and ended up choking on it, it only took a few minutes for the grief to tumble onto the tundra and blow away. I wiped my eyes with my blue bandana, shook my shoulders to even the pack, and carried on. Happy to be walking. Happy, at long last, to feel at home.

In those times when no one was talking—and thankfully, there were a lot of them—I found myself thinking about some of the last conversations Jane and I ever had. By amazing good fortune, our final road trip together—that last springtime journey across the north country, to Ontario—led to incredible discussions. The sort of exchanges that might happen with couples when one partner is passing away slowly, from an illness, when there's no doubt that each conversation should go solely to things worth talking about. We recounted favorite trips—in Seville and Paris and Oaxaca, in the Weminuche and Acadia, the redwoods and Yellowstone. We talked of what had changed about the dreams that launched us some twenty-five years earlier, and what was still the same. Rolling across the prairie—somewhere in western Minnesota, I think it was Highway 10—we talked about the wild. In particular, we talked about getting lost.

Jane had spent years on a search-and-rescue team, helping people missing or injured in the Absaroka-Beartooth Wilderness. On that drive across Minnesota she mentioned how being lost tended to unleash in some people—a lot of people—a crippling sense of dread. A dread that had to do with realizing they weren't in control. And that state of mind, in turn, often led to baffling, even insane behavior. It was the anxiety about what *might* happen, she said, rather than what was *actually* happening, that sent people ambling off in circles. That made them walk off in freezing temperatures with their coats sitting on the ground. That caused them to lose their food, their flashlights, their shelters, their sleeping bags, their packs.

We talked about why that feeling of being out of control, even for thirty minutes, an hour, was so terrifying. On that day, along that stretch of Midwestern prairie highway, it didn't seem that hard to understand. The fantasy of control, after all, had been one of the biggest illusions of our generation. This idea that with enough cash or brains or privilege or looks or piety or technology or stuff sold to us by companies that traded on that very fantasy, we could opt out of hardship and loss.

"But you really can't spend much time in nature," she said, "without seeing the craziness of that." Avalanches run down the mountain. The river floods, gets too high to cross. Lightning hits the ridgeline you're on. The grizzly doesn't give up the trail. And there's never any option but to deal.

* * * *

UP THERE IN THE BEARTOOTHS ON THAT SCATTERING JOUR-
ney, without her, I was thinking about all the ways people lose
their bearings on inward journeys, too. When we're lost inside
ourselves—we're still prone to panic, and at such times, drugs,
booze, or some other kind of isolation can be incredibly appealing. With that in mind, it's interesting to consider that for thousands of years, in every culture on the planet, there's been a sort
of loose blueprint for getting through such scary journeys—
something that grew out of storytellers watching humans experience times of momentous change. The passage always begins
with a loss of identity. That loss of identity is followed by an
often-long, sometimes-excruciating wandering phase—a sense
of having no idea where you are, no idea where you're going. A
sense of being lost.

When something goes wrong out in wild nature—like getting lost—it feels like the world is no longer yours. You've come
unmoored in a strange place, in the land of the bear and the
wind and the rocks. Jane used to say that as you start searching
for clues, as you begin to wander, the trick was to summon the
resolve to breathe through that terrifying state of not knowing.
Over the years, being in the wild had taught both of us to look
such feelings in the eye, to watch them long enough to see clues
that might otherwise be buried in panic. Finding a way out never
took fierce rationalism. It took the calm courage of attention.

I knew that this was also what I needed when wandering

though the dark, thorny fields of grief. Being able to muster attention, forgoing the enormous seduction of escape, offers travelers an essential reassurance. In a way it was just a new twist on that old Greek definition of beauty—beauty as "being of one's hour"—even when the path is baffling. Even when you're utterly, completely lost.

* * * *

AT CHRISTMAS LAKE I HAD A DREAM ABOUT JANE. ONE THAT I kept to myself, puzzling over it the next day as we worked our way north into the heart of the Beartooths. In the dream I was walking with her along the shore of a partially frozen river. All of a sudden, without warning, she jumped off a small bank onto what looked like a solid platform of snow-covered ice. But the shelf gave way, and she fell into the river. I could hear her screaming under the water. Then I was running downstream, frantic, heading for a point just beyond where the ice covered the channel. I was also aware of the real wreck on the Kopka, not believing how such a thing could be happening again. Then I jumped into the river and start searching. Nothing. Soon rescuers showed up, and somehow they turned down the flow on that particular braid of the river, lowering the water level to reveal a long, barrel-shaped tunnel or cave just downstream from where she disappeared. Feeling hopeless, suddenly I heard a shout. And there she was, walking out of the cave.

She went on to tell me how she'd found escape in a small

alcove just above the waterline. Also, that while she was waiting, she'd gotten into some kind of deep meditation state as a survival technique. In the next scene we were in a car, driving away from the river, me in the front passenger seat and her in the back. I turned to ask her about the other river accident, the one on the Kopka. She looked at me with the most serene smile. Told me that we didn't need to get into that right now.

Jane was never specific about where in the Beartooths she wanted her ashes scattered, and there were dozens of options. Lakeshores where we'd sat in the sun with cups of coffee, squinting at distant ridges, trying to figure out how best to cross them; hidden streams where we'd stripped naked after hours of backpacking and laid up to our necks in the cold pools; summits where we'd sat on lichen-covered rocks and eaten salami and apples, a thousand square miles of the world tumbling out to every horizon.

The southern reaches of the range, though, roughly from Line Creek Plateau west to Cooke City, held special meaning for her—partly because of the journeys we'd made there together, and partly from her work with Outward Bound. But also because of time she'd spent here doing search-and-rescue work as a wilderness EMT. Her loaded rescue pack always stood at the ready out in the garage, and when calls came, sometimes at eight or nine at night, saying someone was lost or hurt or unconscious in some faraway rock pile, she changed her clothes, grabbed her radio, and was out the door in minutes.

When she came back from those trips, often well after sunup, she was full of stories: tales of wandering across pockets of tundra in pitch black with a headlamp, of backboarding people with spinal injuries and transporting them to a decent helicopter-landing spot, waiting there for first light, when helicopters could fly; of how family members cried when the search team appeared. She never went on a rescue call without a special box of chocolates made to look like Band-Aids, which she handed out mostly to any kids on the scene, but sometimes to adults, too, trying to ease their worries.

* * * *

TOM, BRIAN, AND I REACHED BECKER LAKE THE MORNING of the fourth day, having lost time when I tried an alternate route I'd heard about but couldn't find. After a night of cold and nearly constant rain—the only such weather of the trip—the wind rounded to the west and the sun broke free. As we topped a small rise at the south end of Becker, the scene took our breath away. The lake shimmered with the deep blue of glacier water, while the shore was dappled with a loose toss of conifers. Beyond the far end, at last within easy reach, was Lone Mountain—the peak we'd been staring at hour after hour on our first two days of walking, high above the Rock Creek Valley. At the best campsite was a yellow tent, which I recognized as belonging to my old friends Kent and his wife Diane. I tossed a loud whistle down the rocks, and with binoculars saw them turn and finally spot us, waving their arms overhead. Their dog Buckley was quicker on the draw. Sensing an important mission, he was already heading toward us at a fast gallop, anxious to herd us home.

* * * *

THE SCATTERING HAPPENED MID-AFTERNOON, JUST AS A TAT-tered sheet of overcast sky pulled apart into clusters of gray-bellied clouds floating through the summer blue. The air smelled of pine and sedge and lake water. We were an eclectic lot: an attorney and his wife, a restaurateur, a retired ranger and his wife, a fellow writer and a judge—all glad to have come for the friend they'd lost, as well as for the one who still remained.

This ceremony was the first done with other people present, as would be the last one, in Yellowstone. It wasn't that I didn't know the power of community: I'd seen it time and again, both in the months following Jane's death, but also years before—how friends, even new friends, really can in times of tragedy take a share of the burden and, in doing so, stem the bleeding of loneliness.

I'd done the first scatterings by myself because those journeys were about me claiming an intimate gift: the chance to go to wilderness on Jane's behalf. By remembering what the Sawtooths and the Wood River and the slickrock country had done for each of us, I was able to begin moving from the feeling that I'd been cheated to a recognition that nothing could take away the life we'd shared. With that gratitude, I began to discern the stepping-stones through grief. The first three scatterings had been about recovery. These last two were about celebration.

We sat in a circle under the arms of an old Engelmann spruce, and I asked if anyone had any Jane stories to share. Janet told of sipping champagne with her in the outback under the stars on New Year's Eve—a memory plucked from one of the many ski treks we'd made with her and Rand, pulling sleds filled with cheeses and game hens and wild rice and cream sauces. She said she still talked to Jane, had long conversations, especially in summer, on her almost-daily walks into the backcountry. Diane said she missed the sight of Jane skiing the two miles from our house into town at ungodly hours of the morning, on her way to work at the café.

As the stories unfolded, some of us cried. But we cried with smiles on our faces. Even all those years after the wreck on the Kopka, Jane's life was binding us to one another. Seven different versions of a good love.

As for me, I decided to tell a story. My favorite story, passed to me years ago by an Ojibwa elder in Minnesota. Since Jane's death, hardly a week passes that I don't think of it.

It was a long time ago in the land of trees. Spirit Woman had given birth to human twins. Now as it happened, it fell to the animal people to care for these babies, and they were committed to the task—doting on them, eager to meet their every need. Bear warmed them through the wee hours by hugging them to her hairy chest. Then each morning at dawn, Beaver came along, taking the babies from Bear and carrying them to the shore of a nearby lake, where she dipped

*them in the water and then set them out in the meadow in
the sun to dry.*

*Then it was Dog's turn. Dog took his job more seriously
than anyone. When flies came along and pestered the babies,
Dog snapped at them to chase them away. When the twins
were cranky, out of sorts with colic, he nuzzled their bellies
with his cold, wet nose and made them laugh. If that didn't
work, he jumped into the air and did all manner of clever
tricks. Deer gave them milk throughout the day. At night the
birds sang them to sleep.*

*But something wasn't right. And one morning Bear
got up the courage to say something about it. "We feed them
and care for them like our own," she said. "But still they don't
stand. They don't run and play." Everyone knew exactly what
she was talking about. "Okay," said Dog, already making a
plan. "Nanabush, the son of the West Wind, is coming tomor-
row. He's smart. He'll know what to do."*

*Sure enough, the next day, Nanabush did come. Because
Nanabush always comes when the animal people need him. He
studied the babies out in the meadow, all the while listening,
nodding his head as the animal people explained the problem.
First of all, he finally told them, you've done a good job taking
care of these human babies.*

*"I think maybe you did too good of a job. The young of
any creature don't grow by having everything done for them.
They grow by reaching, by struggling for what they want."*

But as smart as Nanabush was, he was clueless about how to fix it. So as he'd done countless times in the past, he readied himself for a long journey west, to a certain high peak he knew about—maybe it was right here in the Beartooths—to ask the Great Spirit what to do.

Nanabush left the land of the trees and began the long trek across the prairie, reaching that certain mountain after weeks of hard travel. With no small effort he climbed to the summit, and there summoned Great Spirit. And Great Spirit came. Because Great Spirit always comes when Nanabush calls. After explaining the predicament, Nanabush was told to start scouring the summit of that great mountain for a certain kind of colorful, sparkling stone. "Gather every one of them into a big pile, right here," Great Spirit said. It was a huge job. But Nanabush had been around long enough to know there was no use trying to bargain for something easier. He started collecting, day after day after day, until finally there was an enormous pile made up of every last one of the colored stones.

But what was he supposed to do next? Hour after hour he sat there hoping for some further instruction from Great Spirit. But no word came. Finally, out of boredom, Nanabush began tossing the stones into the air, first one at a time, then big handfuls. He invented games. He learned to juggle. Then one morning, as the sun was poking above the east horizon, he grabbed a big handful of the stones and tossed them high into the air. Only this time, they didn't come down again. This *time they changed, turning from stones into the most beautiful winged creatures Nanabush had ever seen. They were the world's first butterflies.*

Now he knew what he needed to do. He worked his way down the mountain and began the long trip back across the prairie, the whole time surrounded by a flashing, fluttering blanket of butterflies. When he finally got back to the land of the trees, back to the babies, the twins looked up from the grass and were overjoyed. Their arms went up toward the sky, and they were trying their best to catch the butterflies in their chubby hands. Of course that's no way to catch a butterfly. Pretty soon they started crawling after them. A few more weeks passed, and they were on their feet, still reaching, still trying. In time they were walking. And then not so long after that, they were running through the woods and across the meadows, trying to catch even one of those beautiful winged creatures.

And that, say the Ojibwa, is how butterflies taught children to walk.

I told my friends how before I left the storyteller's cottage, she'd put her hand on my shoulder and said that if I told the tale, I should understand something: that her people don't keep it alive because they need to be reminded not to give their children everything they want.

"We pretty much get that," she told me. "We tell the story when we get stuck. When we fall into sadness or anger or lose hope. The story tells us to first heal our relationship with beauty—that beauty will help us start moving again."

When the circle came to an end, when no one had anything more to say, I offered up the silver spoon and the pottery jar, inviting everyone to take part in the scattering of ashes. Each person took the spoon and walked away, disappearing for a time, searching with great care—for the right view, the perfect cast of granite, a certain strength of breeze. Plucking metaphors in the quest for a perfect final resting place for their friend. The only one I actually saw was Diane, standing fifty feet above the shore on a narrow perch of granite; I caught sight of her just in time to see her let loose her measure of ashes, watched them float east and then north, toward the heart of the Beartooths, before finally disappearing.

Mine were cast along the lake, over a patch of cherry-colored monkey flowers. During our summer forays in the high country, monkey flowers were always with us, wrapping alpine streams and lakeshores with ribbons of pink and yellow and scarlet—first in the Sawtooths of Idaho, then up and down the Rockies from New Mexico to Montana. A brilliant little flower thriving in the harshest of climates, a plant that botanical healers have long used to treat sadness and depression, claiming it brings joy to troubled hearts.

RESCUE

The next morning, three members of our group packed up and headed for home; the rest of us moved north. Janet and Rand were planning to carry on with us for the next three days, covering a portion of the remaining sixty miles to Yellowstone, parting company at the western edge of the Beartooths. The weather continued to improve, finally exhaling into one of those perfect days in the mountains that leave you wanting for nothing. It began what would be the finest weather of the summer.

From Becker on, I was finally, fully back in the mountains. The great German philosopher Friedrich Schiller was right to claim—as Jane too liked to say—that people are only completely human when they play. And playing is something I'd done precious little of in the past few years. But now I was playing. Rand, who has a long history of wandering this country, was busy taking stock of things: noting the size of the snowfields at Jasper Lake compared to when he had seen them just two years earlier, calculating the likely geological composition of a high ridge flashing in the afternoon light. Janet, meanwhile, was simply grinning. Smiling at the feel of a warm breeze at nine thousand feet, smiling at the scent of the bluebell and monkey flower gardens that wrapped every stream.

But in mid-afternoon, the talk turned melancholy. The permanent snowfields and glaciers we'd come to know in this area over the years were disappearing, and fast. More significant still, on the high ridges to the south we could see old familiar tufts of whitebark pine, huddled like old women telling stories—no longer green, though, instead turning brown. Dying due to infestations of pine bark beetles, an insect able to survive at these upper elevations thanks to warming temperatures—part of the biggest insect blight ever to hit North America. One that'll probably wipe out the whitebark of greater Yellowstone in the next twenty years.

The Clark's nutcrackers of the region had used these trees for centuries, each bird burying as many as twenty thousand seeds in shallow caches to feed on through the winter. What's more, the tree's nuts remain among the most important foods for grizzly bears; during years of abundant seed crops, a bear may get half her calories from them. It was even more troubling that these grizzly meals were disappearing at exactly the same time another one—spawning cutthroat trout—was dwindling too, the result of the region's streams being blown dry by drought.

I knew then that I was going to miss the whitebarks. Even the kindest months in this country can bring great fits of sleet and hail and snow; on more than one occasion I'd found myself with only one refuge, under the branches of those silvery-barked conifers. Even John Muir, famous for climbing hundred-foot-high Douglas fir trees during windstorms for the chance at a sway ride, found himself on plenty of occasions on his belly under whitebark, peering out through their ropy branches at some outburst of raging weather in the high Sierras.

Beyond gratitude at being able to play again, then, that glum reality was also part of our trek to Yellowstone: the feeling of life shifting, unraveling before it reassembled into something new. Of course the snowfields and the whitebark were only the beginning. The little pika, or rock rabbit, which in summer cuts and dries piles of grass on the high-elevation flats of boulder piles—sometimes enough to fill a bushel basket—was seeing his usual summer crops taken over by less nutritional plants, ones more able to thrive in this warming climate. Soon the pika, too, will disappear from here. Meanwhile to the southwest of where we were walking, on the northern range of the national park, the wet places were drying out—taking with them the Columbia spotted frog. The blotched tiger salamander. The boreal chorus frog.

The question is asked often these days about what future generations will think of us for not doing enough in the face of climate change. But right now it feels like the only thing worse than not doing enough is pretending not even to notice. So the five of us are noticing. Trying to be loyal to some vague feeling that calls us to at least witness the losses—and for me, to promise to miss these things when they're gone.

Maybe the first step in solving climate change is being courageous enough to face our reactions to the mere mention of it— these feelings of being overwhelmed, this rush of sadness and frustration at the thought of something that seems way too complicated to solve. Maybe if we could face all that, if we could grieve, we'd find our way on to what's next.

In the months before this trek, I'd been spending a fair amount of time with twenty-somethings. A couple living with their new baby in a tiny yurt out in Luther—no electricity, not even running water—making their money spring through fall by marshaling a herd of goats across people's property, the goats being magnificent at eating down the noxious weeds that flourish in this warming, drying climate. And then this brilliant Yale-trained architect, who a year after graduation had turned his back on his celebrated New York employer to become a cowboy on the Lazy E L Ranch. And also the daughter of an old fly-fishing friend, gathering organic vegetables from greenhouse growers, carting them in her biodiesel truck to high-end restaurants.

I've often thought these young people were somehow different from the splendid longhairs of my own generation. For one thing, their efforts on behalf of the planet seem less a massive party with an open bar than a modest, slightly buzzed late-night dinner with friends. I imagine them being less prone to the awkward hangover that came to the baby boomers, in that season when we woke up to find the whole world wasn't on board, then tucked our tails between our legs, put on dark glasses, and slipped off into Ronald Reagan's morning in America.

"I think maybe we don't separate things so much," the young man living in the yurt with his wife and baby told me one day. "The wilderness and the city—we don't tend to put them in different boxes."

I told him that made it sound like he and his peers were living their ecologies, trying to make them real instead of just weaving ideas about them. I told him that to people my age, environmental issues can seem like spectator sports—the believers fistfighting with the deniers, and the rest of us convinced we're doing something just by cheering for the right team. He stopped, turned to me, and grinned, ran his hand up across his forehead into his thick black hair.

"Hey, your generation stood on somebody's shoulders, just like mine stands on yours. Maybe you guys lost your way. And yeah, when you did, the whole world suffered. But look around. The dream goes on."

* * * *

THE ONLY TRAILS IN THIS PART OF THE MOUNTAINS, WHEN there are trails at all, are those etched into the tundra by elk and mountain goats and bighorn sheep, their paths as often as not disappearing at the foot of some rocky cliff where humans never go. In some places, mostly along the shores of lakes set in the necks of narrow canyons, there isn't even that; travel there is by virtue of that grand dance backpackers fondly refer to as boulder hopping. While the five of us were past the age of extreme hopping, barely knowing where our feet would land before the need to land them, there were nonetheless moments when a clear path revealed itself across the rocky chaos and we cranked up the pace. At the east end of Otter Lake, Tom was very nearly stranded on a twenty-foot-long ledge. He looked panicked, his eyes darting and flashing, struggling to get control of his breathing. At last he managed it, made it across.

By the west end of Otter Lake, we'd grown fatigued, began picking our steps with extra care. Then it happened. Somewhere behind me I heard a gasp, turned to see Janet sitting in a jumble of rocks with her hand on her ankle and a terrible grimace on her face. By the time I made my way back to her, Rand was unlacing her boots. Even while soaking the ankle in the cold water of the lake, we could see it swelling before our eyes. We were seventeen miles from a trailhead, much of it over tough terrain. There was no cell phone service. Soon it became obvious—we were going to need a rescue. After about an hour or so of resting, Janet told us she was ready to move toward Mariane Lake, a half mile to the west, the first ground flat enough to set up a camp. She insisted on making it under her own power, so we forged a crutch; then Rand started shuttling packs while Brian walked behind her, ready to catch her if she stumbled.

Tom and I, meanwhile, made a fast, steep climb up some four hundred feet of mountain to a high ridge on the slim chance that his cell phone might be able to pull a signal from either Cooke City or the Clark's Fork Valley. After thirty minutes we reached a pinnacle of granite jutting out high above a loose knit of forest, offering views to the south and west that, even in the midst of those dire circumstances, made us catch our breath. In the distance were Index and Pilot peaks, the latter named by trappers who used it as a landmark on their way to the Lamar Valley of Yellowstone. Far to the south lay the awesome, ragged line of the Absarokas, tearing into the sky along the eastern border of the national park. And slightly east of the Absarokas was the wild neck of the Clark's Fork Valley. Tom tried his cell phone several times, holding it over his head and turning it this way and that. Nothing.

On the way down off the ridge, I started plotting the next move. I'd leave Rand with Janet and hike out the seventeen miles to a trailhead east of Cooke City, where Rand's truck was parked, then drive into town and rustle a helicopter. Given the late hour, I imagined I could make eight or nine miles that night, then get up at dawn and walk the remaining distance to the truck, making it to Cooke City by eight or nine in the morning. I told Tom the plan, said that he and Brian could either come along or stay the night at Mariane Lake. He didn't hesitate, telling me that he and Brian would make the fast trip out with me.

Approaching the east shore of Mariane Lake, we found Janet sitting on the bank of a small inlet stream, soaking her ankle. Rand, a former smoke jumper and fire boss for the Forest Service, knew intimately the needs of helicopters and was busy setting camp near a good landing spot. When I told them my plan to go out for help, they resisted, deeply troubled by the thought of me being pulled off this sacred journey. I reminded them that this part of the Beartooths was where Jane often came while volunteering for search and rescue, helping people like Janet, injured in the middle of nowhere. I gave Janet a big hug and whispered in her ear:

"What do you think Jane would want me to do?"

She smiled through her tears, and that was the end of it.

We filled water bottles, offered a quick round of hugs, then Tom, Brian, and I were off, crossing the southern boundary of the lake to begin a steep drop of some five hundred feet through a great jumble of blowdown, heading for the thick woods cradling Russell Creek. It proved a brutal descent, with all sign of the trail obliterated, and so it was a great relief to finally level out in the lodgepole forest south of Russell Lake. By then, it was twilight. This is dense grizzly country, and because we were traveling at such a fast clip it became all too easy to spot rocks and broken conifer stumps hovering in the murky woods and turn them into bears. The good news, I said to the boys, is that grizzlies almost never mess with parties of three or more. By the time we came to rest, it was after dark. We used headlamps to put up the tents in a patch of ghost forest burned in the 1988 fires, covered in blankets of tall brown grass. Then we hung the food bags and fell into an exhausted sleep.

* * * *

WE MANAGED TO BE MOVING AGAIN BY DAWN, FINALLY REACH-ing a pay phone at the Cooke City Exxon station around eight fifteen. We informed the local dispatcher where we were going for breakfast, and at the very moment the omelets were set on the table, a young man came up and asked me to follow him to the fire hall. There an old friend waited, a search-and-rescue volunteer named John Odemeyer. After getting all the details, he called in a helicopter. We headed off in Rand's truck to the land-ing pad at Pilot Creek to wait for Janet's arrival, eating the rest of our breakfast off our laps out of Styrofoam platters with plas-tic silverware. Thirty minutes later, we heard the unmistakable drum of helicopter blades. When Janet hobbled out, helped by still another old friend, an EMT from Red Lodge named Blake Chartier, she took us by surprise with the big grin on her face.

"My God!" she exclaimed. "You wouldn't believe how beau-tiful that country is from the air!"

They climbed into the truck, and Rand drove us back to Cooke City, then turned his red Dodge around to make for Billings, for the hospital, 120 miles away. A few hours later, I telephoned Janet. She told me the ligament that attaches to the outside of her foot was so torqued when her ankle turned that it broke the bone.

I slept lousy that night in Cooke City, unhappy to be in a motel room. Still, it'd been an enormous pleasure to lend help to my friend Janet. The day we arrived in Cooke City, John

Odemeyer had made a generous offer to drive us back into the mountains so we could resume our journey, so the next morning, he picked us up in his Bronco, and after loading our gear began winding up the jeep roads over Lulu and Daisy passes— several miles from where we had hiked out along Russell Creek. And off we went again, bound for Yellowstone. For the final leg of my journey.

* * * *

BACK ON FOOT, CROSSING WOLVERINE PASS ON THE NORTH-east corner of Yellowstone, drifting through still more burned forest, we stumbled into a land silly with wildflowers. Entire meadows blushing with fireweed and bedstraw, fringed by thick patches of sticky geranium and lupine and paintbrush. From camp I drifted down a perfect swimming hole on Wolverine Creek, plunging in and then drying myself in the warm sun atop a fallen log. Dinner was split-pea soup and bread and hummus, and afterward, we climbed a high ridge to the north in the last of the light to glass for wildlife. Eagles and hawks were overhead, eyeing carefully a landscape once useless to them because of the tree cover, now opened by fire into a hunting ground filled with mice and ground squirrels. Woodpeckers hung from the charred trees and dug out insects with their hammer drills.

Later, lying in the tents in the dark, I told Tom about a trip Jane and I had made down this drainage back in 1990, having come by means of a forty-mile hike from the Stillwater River on the northern flank of the Beartooths. We were with good friends, Jim and Nancy Coates, and the night before reaching the valley, we'd settled into a beautiful camp near Lake Abundance. The conversation was golden. The sky was riddled with stars. At one point Jim surprised us with a bottle of Jose Cuervo, and with a little salt and lime it actually tasted great. Which of course is never a good thing when drinking tequila. I overindulged, ending up the next morning greeting the dawn by retching in the willows. "I saw you over there on your knees," Jim told me later. "Hell, I thought you were meditating!"

When I finally donned my pack that morning I was barely running on one cylinder, dreading the thought of walking fourteen miles in eighty-degree heat. To make matters worse, Jane, despite having a good thousand miles on the boots she was wearing, developed a bizarre set of blisters. She moved down the trail like someone walking on hot coals. Together we looked like something a grizzly might drag out of a snowbank in the April thaw.

Jim and Nancy agreed, given our sluggish pace, to make a quick sprint to the trailhead, where they'd take our car to retrieve their van, then return with both vehicles to pick us up. An hour or so after they left us, the manager of the Silver Tip guest ranch drove up in a horse-drawn wagon, heading the other direction. Next to us he halted.

"Are you the two people dying on the trail?"

We hit the trailhead just as darkness was falling, weary as hell but in high spirits. We'd just taken off our packs and settled into lounge mode, when Jane said she thought it would be really funny if I mooned Jim and Nancy as they returned with the vehicles. I thought it was a great idea.

After about twenty minutes, Jane pegged the lights coming up the road as those of our car. Right according to plan, I turned and dropped my hiking shorts, bending over and waiting for the horn to honk and the laughter to begin. The next thing I heard was a window being rolled down, then a strange woman's voice: "Nice cleavage. But do I know you?" It was two women from Colorado pulling over to ask if we knew of any camping sites nearby. Of course my standing as a source of reliable information was compromised. After mumbling an apology, I offered what I knew as far as campgrounds and prayed they'd leave quickly, which they did. Jane found the episode incredibly funny—hilarious, really, judging by the fits of laughter I could hear coming from her the entire time I was struggling to dispense campground information. For years afterward she could pull herself out of a bad mood just by thinking about it.

AT REST IN
YELLOWSTONE

The journey was winding down. Just one more night in the backcountry. With every passing hour, I found myself wishing it wasn't coming to an end. I wanted to keep going, keep walking through Yellowstone for another week or two or three, until the snows of autumn pushed me home. Tom asked if I had any worries about reaching this point, about reaching the end. But by then I'd had a strong glimpse of the life I knew Jane would want for me. I was at the point, I told him, where maybe it was less important to imagine my eyes and ears and nose and skin as portals for her to experience the world, as I did in northern

Canada, than to see them as doorways for making my own way back among the living.

The national park's nature school, known as Expedition: Yellowstone!, was Jane's favorite teaching job—a nearly perfect fit, where kids came brilliantly uncorked by a land beyond their wildest imaginings. It was also a serious classroom. Fourth, fifth, and sixth graders from schools around the country spent months back home learning about the park, and then they boarded busses and rolled off for Yellowstone to see it for themselves. Their experiences were grounded in the latest research of bird and wolf and bear and bison biologists, geologists and volcanologists, plant scientists, historians.

There's nothing better, Jane used to say, than seeing the face of a ten-year-old fresh out of bed at the Buffalo Ranch, walking out to find a pack of wolves cruising up the valley a mere three hundred yards away. Or being high up on Specimen Ridge, standing by as a young boy closes his eyes and runs his fingers over the stone skin of a petrified tree. She worked with incredibly talented people at Expedition: Yellowstone!, many who greatly deepened her own knowledge of ecology and natural history. She'd grown more confident here, able to hatch teachable moments wherever she was, night or day. And like the kids, she too got to wake up to bison ambling up the valley, watch bull elk battle for harems, see pronghorn calves go in a matter of days from wobbly legs to lightning speed.

A few months ago I found a big manila envelope in her office where she kept letters from her students, some of whom kept in touch with her well into their teen years. *Dear Ranger Jane,* wrote Rod from Denver. *Yellowstone is the most awesome place ever. I loved the hikes. Do bison ever need doctors? When I grow up I'm going to be a veterinarian.* Or from Shelly in Bozeman: *Dear Ranger Jane, Thanks for all the neat things you taught us. I liked the web of life game best. I had a dream about geysers. I was sad when I woke up and I wasn't really there.*

Her job in Yellowstone occurred across four months of the year, two of them in spring and two in fall. On her days off, which came in blocks of three, in the early weeks of autumn, either I'd go to Yellowstone or she'd drive two hours back across the Beartooths to Red Lodge. But by October, and continuing through the entire spring season, the Beartooth Highway was closed, which meant one of us faced a five-hour commute. So instead we often met halfway. In September and early October, we showed up with loaded backpacks to hike into the wilderness for a couple days, often near Becker Lake. In early spring we came with skis and chili and bourbon, heading off to some backcountry cabin on the Boulder River or Mill Creek or the Crazy Mountains.

It was hard, the two of us being apart so much, a problem made worse by my own comings and goings. On the weekends she spent in Red Lodge, there was always way too much to do: paying bills, working on the house, doing laundry, mowing the lawn, buying toilet paper, seeing the dentist. But it was different on those rendezvous in the backcountry. By then we'd been together more than a dozen years. We'd struggled through times of little money, helped each other when we were sick, tended friendships, stood together and watched parents suffering and dying. And because of all that, when we got to the outback, we slipped into the relationship with barely a ripple.

* * * *

A SHORT WALK FROM WOLVERINE CREEK, WHERE TOM, BRIAN, and I made our next-to-last camp, the trail came to an abrupt end, obliterated by fallen timber, leaving us to head off cross-country in the general direction of the northern border of Yellowstone. To get there meant first climbing a sharp divide toward Lost Creek. The bad news: it was covered with the mother of blow-downs. There's nothing so tiring, nothing so sure to bring a hiker to the edge of exhaustion, than a blowdown in a mature conifer forest. Years after the fires roared through, when the winds of spring and then autumn were blowing, trees began toppling into a vast hodgepodge of pick-up sticks. Most fell with massive root systems intact, which held the bases of the fallen trunks four to six feet off the ground. Going anywhere meant an endless series of zigzags, mostly up steep inclines. Where the fallen trees were low enough to the ground, we slid over them, doing our best not to come off the other side unbalanced by the packs. Sometimes we clambered up onto the biggest trees—those not spiked with lines of branches—then walked their trunks above the down timber, happy to make forty or fifty feet at a time. Sometimes we crawled. It took nearly two hours to make the first half mile.

As we finally topped the ridge, our hearts sank to find the

slopes on the other side covered with blowdown as far as the eye could see. Broad-shouldered Cutoff Mountain rose two thousand feet above us, the entire cloak of forest that once covered its steep slopes completely burned and toppled, leaving the peak looking more rugged and forbidding than ever. Though we started the day with full bottles of water, there was little left, and from where we were, water was a long way away. Needing to reach the banks of Lost Creek, we headed first toward a ravine lying to the northwest. For no particular reason, though, at the last minute, that choice felt wrong. So I turned the party, and we made our way across still more blowdown toward a similar draw to the southwest. After two hundred yards of the usual brutal going, against all odds, we stumbled across the top end of a section of trail recently cleared by a cutting crew; by no small miracle, it ran all the way to Lost Creek.

Our feet hot and swollen, our tongues thick, we damn near skipped to the place where the trail crossed the creek, kicking off our boots and peeling off our shirts and shorts to submerge ourselves in the foot-deep water. Each of us was wearing an impressive collection of cuts on our legs, some of them still bleeding. I'd been acting as the lunch cook for the expedition, and I pulled out the last of our best ingredients, making fat tortilla wraps out of hard salami and cheddar cheese spiced with yellow mustard. We sat in the shade like schoolboys playing hooky, recounting with enthusiasm our recent trials. When we moved again, it was on clear trails, walking another few miles before setting up camp, near dark, at the border of the park.

Though we didn't know it at the time, this northern line of Yellowstone was about to become ground zero for a sorry side effect of wolf management being given to the states—a handoff that occurred when the animals were taken off the endangered species list just the year before. Wolf hunting had recently become legal. And time and again, packs who were spending nearly all of their days in the park would wander for brief moments across the boundary; having never learned to recognize humans as threats, they would stand a mere hundred or so yards away from the hunters, wearing curious looks on their faces as the gun barrels were leveled. Especially prized by the shooters would be alpha males and females—easy to spot, since they were often the only ones in a pack wearing collars. Fish-in-a-barrel shooting at its finest.

The effect on the population of the park's wolves would be devastating. In a single year, from 2012 to 2013, the population would drop 25 percent, in large part thanks to these reckless wolf-harvest policies of the states. Of course the problem could be eased by establishing so-called "sub-quota" zones along the border, buffer areas where fewer wolves could be taken. But Montana's politicians would have none of it. Even once-respectable organizations like the Rocky Mountain Elk Foundation would drink the Kool-Aid, ignoring the fact that wolves and elk had coexisted here in relative stability for thousands of years.

What is it, anyway, that renders this creature, arguably more than any other, so much bigger than life? For some it's a symbol of all that's wrong with America, while for others, including me, it's a symbol of what's most right. Yet all of us seem happy to ignore the fact that wolves are just another animal—much like us, another predator—doing their level best to make a living in a hard, hard world. For all the attributions of wolves as "super killers" or as animals that "kill for fun," the average lifespan of a Yellowstone wolf is only five years—partly because of territorial disputes and occasional waves of disease, but also because bringing down elk or bison is such a challenge that a lot of them end up dying in the attempt. For every time a park wolf pack brings down a prey animal, on four other occasions, their attempts fail.

What the wolf has done is to give us a more complete, more functional Yellowstone. Thanks to wolves, the grasses on the northern range greatly improved, as elk numbers fell to more sustainable levels. What's more, those same elk shucked their old habits of hanging out in streamside areas where predators can get the jump on them; as a result, there was an enormous increase in beaver colonies on the northern range. Those beavers, in turn, who do so love to dam upstream channels, created habitat for the return of everything from yellow and Wilson's warblers to willow flycatchers and fox sparrows. Grizzly bears, meanwhile, facing multiple food challenges from a changing climate—from that drop in whitebark pine nuts to the dwindling supply of spawning trout in drought-ravaged streams—routinely filch the kills that wolves make, thus scoring dinners of their own. And on, and on, and on it goes.

When wolves were brought home to Yellowstone in 1995—four decades after the brilliant Aldo Leopold called for the animal to be restored to the park—polls suggested the vast majority of Americans, no matter their political stripes, welcomed the event with open arms. And yet even a conservation project as splashy as this one, covered by thousands of media outlets around the world, would—at least outside of wolf territory—soon drop out of public sight. Maybe in some future generation, when healthy wild ecosystems like this one are even more spectacularly rare, wolves will be able to garner more steadfast support. Maybe then we'll find the resolve to say no to those who would binge-slaughter America's wildlife to show their fury at a world that seems hell-bent on leaving them behind. In the meantime, unlike many other species, wolves are more than smart enough, more than hearty enough to survive here in Yellowstone. Even as their kin are shot to pieces a stone's throw from the park's border.

What was especially curious to me on that particular day, with Jane in a jar on my back, was that I felt calmer in the face of all the lunacy. I'd come to know a lot more now about how the world can close in, go dark when you feel powerless and afraid. I too had spent time feeling cheated out of the good old days. I got how awful it can feel, at least at first, when you figure out there's no one to blame.

* * * *

THE NEXT MORNING, SORE BUT UNDAUNTED, WE STARTED THE gentle thirteen-mile walk down the Slough Creek Valley toward a developed campground in Yellowstone, where my friend John would meet us with food for the final dinner. The last day. The sun was full on, ringing in the sky, bringing shimmer and shine to the grasslands of Frenchy's Meadows—so named for a trapper in the late 1800s who set off on a fiery mission to eradicate the grizzly bears of the area, only to end up devoured by one. Though we saw no bears, mostly just elk and bison, the real stars of the show were sandhill cranes, their wild, primitive chortle echoing up and down the valley off and on throughout the morning. At one point Tom and I were locked in a particularly intense conversation when we looked up to find a pair of sandhills not ten yards off the trail, plucking bugs from the branches of a sagebrush.

Besides loons (and, in later years, wolves), the sound of the sandhill cranes, which every spring rang through the skies above our house, was for me the most appealing of all the songs of the wilderness. On several occasions I've been lucky enough to see their fabled mating dance, when a breeding pair comes face-to-face, each then launching into the air again and again with the most graceful hops and jumps, fluttering softly back to the ground. For the Greeks, and later the Romans, the dance of the cranes was said to be a celebration of the joy of life.

The walk was one of the finest in many years. The terrain offered less a hike than a sweet amble, one that matched perfectly the easy mood of Slough Creek, falling to the south slowly, flush with meander. Once again I found myself revisiting that Aboriginal idea of the dead being able to experience the world through the senses of the living. On that last day in Yellowstone, I was really hoping it was true. Because if it is, Jane would've wrapped herself around that trek like a long-lost friend. John was waiting for us about three miles out, eating his lunch on the trail; together the four of us made the final push to the campground. He'd gone to incredible lengths to give us a good welcome, and after a long plunge in Slough Creek, he served up beer and venison chili and salad and Dutch oven cornbread, and we ate until it seemed we'd never have to eat again. Late in the night, after we'd gone to bed, Martha arrived. Doug—my canoeing partner in the Thelon River country of Canada—would find us the next morning at six thirty, arriving in time to join us for the final trek to the ceremony site.

On first planning this trip, I'd intended to have the last scattering just west of the main Lamar Valley. But on that last morning, it just didn't feel right. I found myself wanting to be farther upstream, within view of the old Buffalo Ranch, where Jane had worked as a ranger for so many years. The place where, in the 1830s, the wonderfully literate trapper Osborne Russell laid down on his elbow beside the Lamar River, writing in his journal how he wished he could remain there for the rest of his days. Changing the plan, though, meant that instead of walking three miles from the Slough Creek Campground, it would be closer to five. I told the group, feeling a bit sheepish. But no one seemed to mind.

It'd been raining off and on all through the night, but by dawn, most of the storm had moved on, leaving only gray sky. We hit the trail before seven, strolling out of the campground and then up the highway, the air filled with the smells of Yellowstone:

wheatgrass and patches of Douglas fir, sagebrush and bison dung and an occasional whiff of sulfur. On reaching the west end of the valley, we descended to the Lamar River, traded hiking boots for water sandals, then forged across the sixty-foot-wide flow to a small delta on the south side. Once I settled on a spot for the ceremony, Doug pointed out that I'd chosen a place exactly halfway between a bald eagle nest and an osprey nest. Just up the valley was the Buffalo Ranch, so-named for having served as cowboy central in the early 1900s for the effort to bring wild bison back from the edge of extinction. It would later become a cluster of restored cabins, a cookhouse, and a classroom. And for parts of seven years, it had been Jane's home away from home.

She and I had been off and on in Yellowstone for twenty-three years, and for the last eighteen, Yellowstone had been just beyond our back door. The place soaked into us slowly, revealing some new weave in every season: on top of mountains, in the bottom of canyons, in the swells of these savannah hills. Over the years, we'd left the roads with our packs on and waded knee-deep across rivers, eaten dinner in the shade of lodgepole forests, slept with grizzlies. And as time passed, we'd come to revere this park: the curious look of earth pushing out big pours of boiling water; the spring light on the sage fields of Lamar; the fluty ring of bugling elk in the fall. Even the smells were oddly filling—sometimes like black pepper and lemon peels; sometimes like eggs and toast.

* * * *

ONCE AGAIN, ONE LAST TIME, THE CLOUDS BEGAN TO GIVE
way, revealing patches of something close to autumn blue. We
sat on the ground in a circle, at which point I invited my friends
to share thoughts or memories of Jane. Doug, looking more sad
than I'd ever seen him, told us that the Lamar Valley had always
been a big part of the work he did as a biologist, that he'd never
again set eyes on the place without thinking of her. Once everyone had a chance to speak, I told them that this place, more than
any other in the American West, was where two of the things
Jane loved best came together: wild nature, and the chance to
share it with children. From here she had set off with her young
charges across the Lamar Valley, making long treks with them
toward the Buffalo Plateau. Some days they'd fanned out into
the Norris Geyser Basin to test pH in the thermal features, or
headed for Mammoth to study the travertine terraces. On several
occasions, she'd called me from a pay phone near the trailer she
lived in at Tower Junction, telling me how she couldn't get inside
because of a big bison blocking her way.

The whole of the Lamar Valley seemed at ease that day,
gently animated: Blue bunchgrass and junegrass and milk vetch
trembled in a light breeze. Just up the valley, loose gatherings
of bison were lowering their heads and pulling up mouthfuls of
grass, chewing for a minute or two, then stepping on.

We sat for a few minutes in silence. Then I explained to
my friends how, on this trip, it occurred to me that embracing
Jane in the present meant letting go of her in the past. I thanked
them for being the ones who early on carried me back to the

wilderness—to the river and the tundra; for quaffing beer with me on summer nights under the stars, for hearing on countless occasions some new version of the nature of my sadness.

I explained how, on this trip, it occurred to me that embracing Jane in the present meant letting go of her in the past. I thanked those friends for being the ones who had early on carried me back to the wilderness—to the river and the tundra; for quaffing beer with me on summer nights under the stars; for hearing on countless occasions some new version of the nature of my sadness. As if on cue, the last of the gray clouds drifted apart to drench us with sun, washing the entire Lamar Valley with light. Just to the north, from somewhere high up on the steep, grassy slopes, a pair of coyotes called out with abandon, launching into a lively call-and-response of yips and howls.

At the end of the ceremony, I pulled out a sheet of paper with a few lines on it from Wendell Berry—a passage I found a year after Jane's death, pasted into one of her journals:

And there at the camp we had around us the elemental world of water and light and earth and air. We felt the presences of the wild creatures, the river, the trees, the stars. Though we had our troubles, we had them in a true perspective. The universe, as we could see any night, is unimaginably large, and mostly dark. We knew we needed to be together more than we needed to be apart.

When the time came to scatter the ashes, each of us was left to simply find our own appealing place in those vast, open meadows. For Doug, it was a spot near a big bison wallow, the bare ground layered with course brown hair. John, on the other hand, picked a patch of grass in perfect line of sight with the bald eagle's nest. I went toward the river, finding a low point on the delta. The following spring, the floods would come, carrying Jane's remains on to the Yellowstone, then the Missouri, then the Mississippi, then the Gulf of Mexico.

It was a brilliant finish. In part, I believe, because there's no place on earth like Yellowstone's Lamar Valley. It was here that the American bison was nursed back from the brink of extinction. And here too that, a century later, wolves would take their first steps back into the wild, after being absent for some seven decades. Both run free today, loping or howling or snoozing amidst eagles and ravens and grizzlies and otter and fox. It's in the Lamar, too, that every May, pronghorn fawns, as well as bison and elk calves, are born, the latter by the hundreds—babies rising on wobbly legs, soon to walk, then to run.

When she was working for the Park Service nature school, this was where Jane could be found most every morning, especially during the month of May—an eager woman surrounded by eager children. There she and her students would stand huddled against the chill, staring across these meadows, whispering and gasping and giggling. And every now and then, just looking at one another wide-eyed, feeling lucky. Knowing what a good thing it was to be smack in the middle such a wild place. Chosen ones, they were, witnessing for the whole world that unforgettable spill of new beginnings.

EPILOGUE

As I write this, in early February, the creek that rolls past my back door is frozen fast, little sign of it save the wide path it carved though the belly of the valley long ago, in the time of ice. My experience of this time of year has completely changed since Jane's death. Not that I haven't always liked winter—schussing down untracked slopes on telemark skis, hooking tow ropes to cars with friends and pulling each other down old forest roads at dubious speeds. But now I spend a fair amount of time simply taking in the woods. Sometimes, during storms, I watch whitetail deer coalescing into lines, breaking trail through the deep snow. Small familiarities, akin to the little pieces of miracle that so comforted my mother, and at the same time a part of the grand stories Kenneth Rexroth talked about—pieces of the myths that make us human. The tragedy has left me feeling more aligned with that Inuit notion Jane and I ran across in the Arctic—the one that claims the whole world can be comprehended by paying attention to the relationships at your feet.

I also find myself trying to figure things out—childlike things of little consequence, like just how long a bald eagle is willing to sit on the cottonwood branch outside the house and scan the creek for fish before he gives up the effort and tries someplace else. It's in the woods just beyond my door where I'm likely to recall that life as we know it wouldn't even arise in the first place, unless it also passed away.

Each morning now, all through the winter, there arrives to the edge of the creek a plain little bird—the dipper, jumping off blocks of ice in even the worst weather to pluck larvae from the bottom of the stream, then back up onto the ice again, where she bobs up and down for a time, looking like a little kid about to wet her pants because she's got something important to say. Jane and I used to pretend the dipper we saw across our fourteen years together in this house was the same bird. We called her Darlene.

For reasons I don't fully understand, winter, if not my favorite season, is in these days the one I'm most drawn to. On every night of cloudless sky, Orion and Gemini and Libra come rolling overhead, through heavens so clear I can see starlight shimmering in the forest. A time well after the end of things, and long before they begin again. When every morning I stand in the living room, arms down, and my face inches away from the east-facing window, breathing in and breathing out, considering one more time the right kind of devotion needed to conjure from that snow and ice the buds of spring.

As so often happens when someone dies, especially someone relatively young and strong and full of fire, in the years following the accident, there came to those of us who loved Jane a somewhat tilted vision. It was a kind of delightful penchant for elevating her courage, her astonishing enthusiasm, to dimensions more rightly suited to the gods. We spent countless seasons being both hugely thrilled and deeply saddened by our bedazzling memories of her laughter, her kindness. But Jane didn't live in some kind of paradise of ease and contentment. Like any of us, she was never completely free of doubt, or fear, or uncertainty.

It's been good for me to see this. To reach a point where I can know her again as fully human. Among the greatest gifts she gave, after all, had nothing to do with perfection. Rather, it was the sweet reassurance, the simple boost of spirit that comes from having known someone who managed to see the mythical shining through the mundane.

* * * *

THERE'S GOOD NEWS THESE DAYS, MIXED IN WITH ALL THE craziness, as we push together into this new millennium. But then I suppose that's the way it's always been. America's

twenty-somethings—the goat herders, the young woman shuttling local organic produce, even a group of young African
Americans in the Yerba Buena section of San Francisco, "grinding for the green"—keep reminding me that we still have choices.
Close to home, hundreds of people are making heroic efforts to
establish critical wildlife migration corridors, including a pas-
sageway from Yellowstone through the Canadian Rockies all
the way to the Yukon. Meanwhile the old McLaren Mine near
Cooke City, which has been leaking deadly poison into a major
watershed at the edge of Yellowstone for more than 120 years, is
now nearly reclaimed. Windmills are going up on the highline.
Little kids are running around Yellowstone, deliriously happy.
And in my hometown of Red Lodge, a nature camp has been
started in Jane's honor. Now every summer kids get the chance
to traipse through meadows of phlox and forget-me-nots, kneel
on the banks of mountain streams, shoulder their packs and set
off on the same trails she roamed all those years.

And there's something else, too. Something truly amazing.
Terry Tempest Williams once said about grief that it "dares us to
love once more." In the spring of 2013, I took that dare. I met a
remarkable woman from Portland named Mary Clare—a social
psychology professor, a listener, a champion of diversity and justice. And beyond that, a survivor of her own runs of heartbreak
and calamity. We would fall in love in these uplands of the northern Rockies, and also wandering that great Northwestern city of
hers, amidst the azaleas and roses, under the London plane trees
of Laurelhurst Park.

From the very beginning, we walked, walked everywhere. And six months after we met, on a brilliant day in August, we walked to Becker Lake—that place in the Beartooths where Jane's ashes had been scattered four years earlier. Standing on a ridge high above the eastern shore of the lake, Mary's hand in mine, I opened my mouth and called out into a warm southern breeze.

"Jane," I said. "This is Mary!"

And far below, for a minute or so afterward, there was this dazzling little miracle of wind and water and light running up the south end of the lake. We married the following winter, on Rock Creek, on a morning in January when the dipper was flitting from ice floe to ice floe, and the sun seemed like a village bonfire hanging in the air, lighting fourteen inches of fresh snow.

Our lives too, like every life, are unfolding as wilderness. On any given day, there's both beauty and chaos standing together, just as the Paiute said they would. In some ways, the miles we're traveling together now have been sweetened by our wounds—by each of us having learned beyond the shadow of a doubt that nothing lasts forever. It isn't really fear that rises from such notions, such feelings of impermanence—at least not on our good days—but rather a simple appeal for presence. An invitation to life. And when we accept, there often comes a feeling of being on the finest, brightest of paths—free of future, unshackled by past. All of life encompassed in a single step. And then another. Strung together like pearls, in our long, precious journey from beautiful to goodbye.

ACKNOWLEDGMENTS

This book could not have been written without the support of an extraordinary group of friends, family, and colleagues. Thanks especially to Mark and Gin, for a friendship that not only lifted me when I was broken, but in the end convinced me that I could once again begin to run. Also to Jane's niece, Abby, my brother, Jim, as well as to all the kindhearted people of Red Lodge, Montana. Enormous gratitude too to those who helped craft the narrative: My agent, Nancy Stauffer, for her brilliant insights into the nature of the tale, as well as for her many years of steadfast encouragement. To Dan Smetanka at Counterpoint, for his abundant enthusiasm and masterful editing. And to the spectacularly gifted faculty of the Rainier Writing Workshop.

Lastly, my enduring love and respect to my precious wife, Mary: For her luminous spirit and her dazzling mind. For the way she loosed a gentle breath across my heart, blowing frail embers into lasting flame. And finally, for the way she offered up so gracefully a great measure of the courage needed for two people, each having borne a feast of calamity, to join hands, and begin again.

ABOUT THE AUTHOR

Over the past twenty-five years Gary Ferguson has established himself as an expert chronicler of nature, having written for a wide variety of publications from *Vanity Fair* to *The Los Angeles Times*. He is the author of nineteen books on science and nature, including the award-winning *Hawk's Rest*. He is also a highly regarded keynote speaker at conservation and outdoor education gatherings around the country and is currently on the faculty of the Rainier Writing Workshop Masters of Fine Arts program at Pacific Lutheran University.